Ghosts
of
Block Island

by
Fran Migliaccio

With photography by Marea Mott

Fran Migliaccio

SAN: 2 5 7 – 3 5 1 2

Copyright © 2005 by Frances Huggard Migliaccio
Published October 31, 2005
Reprinted December 2006
ISBN 0-9773639-0-2

Published by:
Frances Huggard Migliaccio
P.O. Box 412
Block Island, RI 02807

$14.95 US

To Rally
and
in loving memory
of
Edrie Dodge

ACKNOWLEDGMENTS

THIS BOOK could not have been completed without the support, efforts and expertise of the following people. I am exceedingly grateful to every one of them:

Johno Sisto, owner of Book Nook Press, for his encouragement in the early stages of the project.

Peter Wood, for initial publication of many of these stories in *The Block Island Times*.

Elizabeth Dixon and Peter Wood, for their suggestions in shaping the narrative.

Marea Mott, the unerring "eye behind the camera," for the originality of her vision and for her initiative and willingness to forge ahead, camera in hand, in the dead of a cold and snowy winter, to create images for this book.

Susan Filippone, for the layout, graphic design, suggestions for photos to be used, valuable editorial input, myriad of creative ideas, and general enthusiasm.

Bruce and Peggy Montgomery for their continued publication of these stories in *The Block Island Times*, creative ideas, talent scouting, moral support and assistance in getting the project underway.

Kelly Walsh, for her careful review of the chapter on Lynn's Way.

All those who gave permissions for photography or shared their photos and artifacts:

The Block Island Historical Society; Champlin and Lisa Starr; Lucinda and David Morrison; the Mott family; Suzann and Frank Walsh, and other owners of Lynn's Way; Michael Finnimore; The Nature Conservancy.

All who generously shared their stories and experiences with me.

Rally, for starting it all.

TABLE OF CONTENTS

LIST OF ILLUSTRATIONS

Front cover: Summit House, Block Island, ca. 1905. In foreground, Thelma Smith, her sister and an unidentified person. Courtesy of Morris Holton, husband to Thelma; courtesy of Robert M. Downie.

A Ghostly Beginning

MY ARRIVAL ON BLOCK ISLAND is a ghost story of sorts. While other people have had reasons, even compulsions, to come to Block Island, I had none. I had driven down from my home in Wenham, Massachusetts to visit friends in Connecticut for a late November weekend. My friends have a house on one of Block Island's beaches; citing the gorgeous, though cold, weather, they proposed an Island weekend.

I didn't particularly want to go. I knew that Block Island would be gray, too quiet, offering no social or commercial interaction: shut down with the no-nonsense finality of a summer pageant turned dark and still, devoid of the bright colors and noisy people that made it live and breathe. The stage-set shops and eating establishments would be glumly anonymous, perhaps boarded up, abandoned by owners and stagehand staff who fled south at the first wintry New England nip in the air.

But, in the interest of good sportsmanship, "Yes, let's go to Block Island!" I said enthusiastically. A drive to Westerly and a 15-minute flight found us rescuing my friends' "island car" from the uneven, hilly and overcrowded terrain that is the Block Island Airport long-term parking lot.

We made a trip to the grocery, much more of a social event on Block Island than it would be on the mainland. Here, people stop to chat in leisurely fashion and often at some length. Even in the smallest town in the smallest state, residents may not see each other for days on end, and even if they do, there's always something to talk about. Our buying expedition brought news of a party at the National Hotel that evening. "Might as well go," we all decided.

The National Hotel is the most prominent building on Water Street. Its height, surmounted by a cupola and flagpole, its white façade and its long front porch, are readily discernible to visitors who arrive at Old Harbor by ferry. The National was, in a sense, brought back from the dead. First built in 1888, the National burned in July 1902; all that remained was a chimney. The same fire claimed four other buildings. The New National House was built on the old foundation in 1903 by Island builder Frank Hayes. It went up at record speed, opening for business the summer after the old hotel had burned.

Three decades later, the National was severely damaged by the raging hurricane of September 21, 1938, which brought winds of 150 miles per hour from the southwest with no warning. Structures on every part of the Island were blown apart: "Block Island looked as though it was lifted out of the sea and dropped down with a thud...Every barn on the Island is demolished. Every hotel, and there are nearly a dozen, is badly damaged," reported the *Providence Journal* of September 23. Hurricane Carol, on August 31, 1954, bashed the Island with winds of 135 miles per hour. A guest at the National, John Northway, reported that the building and its beds shook all night with each gust of wind, and the roof sprang leaks all along the east side. "The water was pouring in and around the front door in torrents," he wrote. Guests were assured by William P. Lewis, the state senator from Block Island who was also owner of the National, that the hotel had been built to sway rather than break in strong gales. Mr. Lewis admonished all guests to stay inside for their own safety.

On the November night in 1986 when my friends and I visited the National, it was full of life and seemed in good enough shape for an old wooden building. As we walked up the front steps, we heard a band playing inside; the only shaking came from many pairs of dancing feet.

We opened the door. A big man wearing a parka, obviously on his way out, stood aside and held the door for us as we came in. My friends recognized him: "Rally!" — they pronounced it "Raleigh" — "where are you going?"

"Oh, I've been here about an hour," he shrugged. "Had a couple of Diet Cokes, decided I might as well go home."

"Come back inside for awhile," they urged. Rally turned around and trooped dutifully back. Our group commandeered a table and spent a convivial evening talking, dancing, having some drinks. Rally stuck with his Diet Coke. "I haven't had a drink in nine years," he told me. "One day I decided to quit, and I never went back."

We swapped life stories. He invited me to return to the Island. We started dating.

That was in 1986.

Rally and I have always agreed that there was something uncanny, perhaps even supernaturally ordained, about our meeting. It was a confluence of unlikely events. I had not wanted to be on the Island that weekend, yet I was. The November party at the National Hotel was a delightful oddity, a rare occurrence for Block Island in the 1980s or even now. Rally, the non-drinker, wasn't in the habit of going out at night, yet he was there; he had taken an evening nap, then gone to the National as an afterthought, to humor some friends who were playing in the band.

Our brief passage in the doorway of the National that evening — I on my way in, he on his way out — seemed like a wisp of a chance of a happening. A ghost of a chance. Two minutes either way, we would not have met.

Befitting our odd luck in being together, we married a year later, on Hallowe'en. A few months after that, we acquired a black cat.

12

From the very start of our relationship, Rally spoke of the haunted old farmhouse that stood next door to his own, newer, house on Block Island. "It really is haunted," he insisted with utter conviction, and proceeded to tell me several of his own experiences with the host of ghosts there.

As he told me his stories and repeated them to people on the Island, other people's stories began to surface, of ghosts, or seemingly supernatural events. I wrote them down and began to publish them in *The Block Island Times*. Readers came forward with more Block Island ghost stories. The stories ran in the paper for several years. I was surprised; I had thought that readers would find the tales a frivolous diversion and would laugh at them (as many did), but there seemed to be real interest. Most people who had ghost stories were eager to share them, even though some storytellers disavowed any belief in ghosts.

In the fall of 1992, at the request of the organizers of the Harbor Church's annual Heritage Dinner, I hosted an after-dinner program of ghost stories, told by those who had experienced them. At the end of the evening, two "ghosts" — created by me from styrofoam and sheets, and sent rappelling down wires rigged by friend and master craftsman Brian Schrauf — whooshed down from the balcony, over the heads of the audience, to disappear through the two doorways at the front of the sanctuary. But those were fake ghosts, and we all knew it.

Here are the stories of, perhaps, real ghosts, as they were told to me.

The people who have shared their stories are interesting in themselves. Block Island is a crossroads that has been found, traveled, and lived in by many ruggedly individual souls: some famous, many not; many gifted, some eccentric; most caring deeply about the Island for a variety of reasons. All of these people have made their contribution to the life here. Perhaps the information I've written about these storytellers will help answer the questions, often posed by visitors, of who has passed through Block Island, who has come here or chosen to live here, and why? The living people, their stories, and their ghosts will, I hope, provide readers with a slice of life on Block Island as I found it. It continues to be an endlessly fascinating place.

SUMMER RETREAT — OR SUMMER HAUNT?

I AM RALLY'S THIRD WIFE. When he was married to his second wife, Diana, the couple spent a great deal of time on Block Island, at the old farmhouse just up the hill from our present home.

The old house was a farmhouse built by members of the Sands family on land that had been apportioned to James Sands, one of the 16 settlers from Massachusetts who purchased shares in the Island and came here to live in 1661.

The house was built and added onto during the course of a century. The earliest part of the building is the back portion; the newer, more spacious front rooms were added in the mid-1800s. During the early 20th century, the house was known as Summit House, a summer hotel that offered meals of produce and meats raised in the farm's surrounding fields and orchards.

From 1957 to 1996, this house was owned by Diana's family: first her mother, Jean Beck, and later a brother, John Beck. During those four decades, the house was widely known as the Beck House, and this is how Rally has always referred to it.

When Jean Beck owned the house, Rally and Diana often came to Block Island from their home in nearby Connecticut, spending weekends or summers and, once, an entire year, in the old house. Rally and Diana generally brought their young daughter, Lisa, to the Island, along with an entourage of family dogs — an array of Tibetan terriers and a 130-pound, long-haired German Shepherd named King — and two cats.

On an August day in 1970, Rally and Diana were staying at the old house and painting the living room, a large, welcoming space with a fireplace and a north-facing window.

"It was a hot day," remembered Rally. "We'd each opened a cold beer, and we'd each had about half a can.

"Suddenly, the room got cold and damp. It felt like a fog bank. I went to the door, but there was no fog, not even a cloud. Outside, it was bright and sunny.

"'I think we have a visitor,' Diana said quietly. She was like that — psychic, very sensitive to supernatural things.

"'Aah, don't worry, Diana,' I told her. 'If he gets fresh with me, I'll get even with him in the next life!' or some stupid remark like that.

"The room stayed cold and damp for awhile. We sat and waited. Then, the cold passed through and the room got hot again, back to normal, just as it had been before.

Diana looked at me and gave a little shrug. 'Guess he's gone,' she said, and started painting again. I picked up my paintbrush again, too, and took a sip of my beer.

"Diana picked up her beer, and took a sip — then, all of a sudden, she ran out of the room, into the hall lavatory. She was coughing and chok- ing; I didn't know what was wrong.

"'What's the matter?' I called, and started after her — I was worried!

"'My beer!' was all she could say, and she started to vomit.

"'Your beer? What's wrong with your beer?'" I asked her, but she couldn't answer.

"I went into the living room, picked up her can of beer, and took it into the lavatory. I poured it into the sink, and it was a thick, green slimy mold, with a horrible, foul stench! You wouldn't believe how bad it smelled!

"Now, that beer had been perfectly good before, just like mine. They were both fresh when we opened them and started to drink them. Beer doesn't go bad, just like that! But something turned the beer in that can to slime. Figure that one out!" concluded Rally.

THE MAN IN THE ROCKING CHAIR

B RISK, FRIENDLY, A BUNDLE OF sheer, unstoppable energy, and a fellow soprano in the Block Island Ecumenical Choir, Edrie Dodge knows more about Block Island than most people. She grew up on the Island and has long family roots and lots of relatives here. She is unafraid to take on any project, whether it involves learning a new skill, remodeling her house or serving as a community leader. During the years I have known her, she has been the prime organizer of the Harbor Church's Roll Call Dinner (the best community dinner in the world!), guiding force behind the church's annual raffle of a handmade Block Island quilt, president of the ecumenical choir, and president of the American Legion Ladies Auxiliary. That's just the tip of the iceberg, and she improves each organization as she goes, leaving meticulous records and a smoothly working enterprise for her successor to take over.

Edrie ran the school cafeteria for 19 years. After that, she worked as a postal clerk 13 years, then served as the Island's postmaster for eight. (She staunchly refused to call herself the "postmistress." The job was "postmaster," and that was that.)

Edrie is married to Willis Dodge, a direct descendant of one of Block Island's 16 founders, Trustrum Dodge. Now "retired" at a pace that would prove daunting to many, Edrie and Willis operate a B&B called Sunset Hill and love to travel as much as they can when they're not busy with their retirement.

I thought that Edrie, of all people, might know of an Island ghost story. To my delight, she gave a brisk nod when I asked her. "I certainly do," she replied:

"One evening, my mother, Annie Hall, and I were sitting in the living room of our house on Sunset Hill. I was about 25. I was sitting in a chair next to the rocking chair. I happened to glance over at the rocker, and I saw a man sitting there. He was a stranger, and he was wearing a black suit. He hadn't been there just a few minutes before, and it wasn't at all apparent how he'd gotten there. He hadn't knocked on the door, or come in through any door; he was just there.

"I'd never seen this person before, and I haven't seen him since, but I remember just how he looked. He was tall and thin, with a thin face and high cheekbones. He had dark hair that was shiny and slicked down as if it had been greased. I got a strange feeling, just looking at him – and how!

"As I sat there and watched him, he looked back at me and grinned — but he didn't make a sound. I guessed what was happening.

"'Ma,' I said, 'Do you see this man who's sitting here in the living room with us?'

"My mother looked up at me, and looked all around the room. 'No,' she told me, after a moment.

"But the man was still there, rocking in the rocking chair. 'Well, Ma,' I said to her, 'Look at that rocker and tell me if it's rocking.'

"She looked over at it. 'Yes, it is,' she told me, 'but there's nobody in it.'

"But the man in black was still there, rocking in that rocking chair.

"Now I'd always heard that when you see a ghost – and I'd guessed that this man was someone from another world — you're supposed to ask them what they want. My Aunt Mabel had told me that. So I turned to this man, and I asked him, 'What do you want?'

"That man turned toward me when I said that, and just *grinned* at me — a great big grin, from ear to ear — and just kept looking at me, with this grin on his face. I didn't know what to make of it. But I just kept looking back at him, and finally I said, 'I think you're in the wrong place.'

"And with that — he just disappeared into the air!

"I never saw him again, and as far as I know, he never came back," concluded Edrie.

THE PHANTOM STEED OF BLACK ROCK

"I DON'T BELIEVE IN GHOST STORIES," asserted Fred Benson, then a keen-minded and — except for his use of a walker — relatively robust 95 years of age.

Fred was one of Block Island's most prominent and best-loved citizens. Born in Boston in 1895, he was placed in an orphanage at age four. In 1903, he was sent as a "home boy" to Block Island, to live at the Pilot Hill farm of Gurdon A. Millikin. Block Island became Fred's home, and he remained at the Millikin farm most of his life.

He attended school on the Island, as stipulated by his release from the orphanage, and during his long life probably did every type of work available. Blessed with a huge physique, great strength, good health and good looks, Fred worked at ditch digging, construction, commercial fishing, clamming, cement work, ice packing, marine salvage, and undertaking. He played baseball with the hotel teams during summers, coached the school baseball team, became a first aid instructor, served as the first captain of the Block Island Rescue Squad, and was elected to five terms as president of the Block Island Chamber of Commerce.

He opened his own car repair business, the Square Deal Garage, then retired to join the Block Island School faculty and teach industrial arts. He taught for 14 years.

When Fred won some money in the Rhode Island lottery, he threw a chicken and lobster barbecue for his many friends, who subsequently contributed a total of $6,000 to establish the Frederick J. Benson Scholarship Fund. An annual chicken barbecue is still held every summer to benefit the scholarship fund. The fund, overseen by a committee, has grown over the years and is awarded annually to a Block Island School student.

When I became acquainted with Fred, in his mid-90s, he was the local representative for the state's Division of Motor Vehicles. He tested and approved applicants for driver's licenses, and I got my first Rhode Island driver's license from him, after taking the exam in the tiny office that had been carved out for him in the space occupied by our local bank, The Washington Trust Company. Surrounded by photographs, memorabilia, awards, citations, paperwork, newspaper articles and much more, Fred held court in this office every day, welcoming all visitors, especially children, to his precinct. He was always ready for company and good talk, and he always had candy to share.

Fred once said, "I don't know where I will go when I leave this earth, but if they are as good to me there as they have been here, I know I will be happy!" Fred died in 1995, shortly after he had reached his hundredth birthday.

That day in 1990, when he was talking to me about ghosts, Fred followed up his declaration of non-belief by describing a spooky aspect of surf casting — a sport at which he excelled — at Black Rock.

"Sometimes, when you're fishing down off Black Rock at night, it's easy to believe there's someone else there," he allowed. "I've been down there many a night, all alone, and heard a thump or plop in the water, not a fish, but another sound entirely. Some nights I would have sworn there was somebody right behind me, making that noise. I'd be sure I could sense somebody there! And I'd look around, but there was never anybody.

"After awhile, I'd realize that the sound was just water — nothing more — splashing against one of the rocks behind me in a certain way that sounded like a person. There's nothing unusual in that! So I don't believe people when they tell ghost stories.

"People have said that I wouldn't be afraid of the Devil!"

While I doubted that Fred would ever have to face up to Lucifer, he did go on to tell me a story about one of his visits to the old Sprague house, near Mitchell's Pond: "I used to go and visit the Spragues, L. David and his wife, about every week," Fred remembered. "They didn't have much, so I'd take them candy and tobacco.

"In 1914, a four-masted schooner, the *Jacob S. Winslow*, had come in near Black Rock with all her sails set, and run aground. Over three days, she broke up and went to pieces; the Block Island Power plant was later built out of lumber from that boat.

"At that time, I was doing some writing for a periodical, so I went down to visit the Spragues and find out if they knew any more than I already knew about the *Winslow*. It was just after noon when I got there. We got to talking — Sprague didn't know much more than I did about the wreck — and after awhile, it got on toward dinnertime. Mrs. Sprague asked me to stay to dinner.

"It was winter time, so it got dark early.

"I didn't want them to go to any kind of trouble for me, and I knew they didn't have much money, but they made it plain they really wanted me to stay, so I did. Mrs. Sprague went into her kitchen, and in a very short time we had fried pork chops, beans, potatoes, biscuits, chocolate layer cake — there was lots of food! I still don't know where all that food came from!

"After dinner, I sat at the table with them awhile. Mrs. Sprague and I were sitting together, talking — and I heard a sound. It was the sound of a horse galloping, very near the house. It started in the distance, then got louder, then faded away again. And then it came back, getting louder and fading, two or three times. When it was loud, we almost couldn't hear ourselves talk — and finally I stopped talking to listen to it, wondering where it was coming from. I hadn't seen any horses around there on any of my visits.

"When I stopped talking, Mrs. Sprague just looked at me and put a hand on my arm. 'Don't mind,' she told me. 'It's nothing we don't hear all the time here.' After awhile, the galloping faded away for the last time.

"There is no way a horse could have galloped through the yard of that house, as close to the house as I heard it. One side of the yard was thick brush, another side was very tall grass, and on a third side was a drop-off right down to the pond.

"Yet — I heard it.

"But, as I said, I don't believe in ghost stories."

The phantom steed redux

Well, Fred Benson beat me to it!" exclaimed West Side Road resident Arthur Rose. "I have a story about that house over near Mitchell's Pond, too!"

Yet — Arthur's story is really not the same as Fred's.

"I was born and brought up over on the south side of the Island, in the white house between Lakeside Drive and Fresh Pond next to Ralph and Elva Derby's house," Arthur told me. "L. David Sprague and his wife, Miss Ida, were our neighbors.

"Now, L. David had a horse and buggy that he used to drive into town, and most days, on his way in, he'd see me in our yard and he'd stop and ask me if I wanted to ride in with him. 'Better go and ask your mother, to make sure it's all right,' he always said. So, I'd go ask my mother, and she'd always say yes. I used to go just about everywhere with him.

"On one of those days, L. David and I drove into town in his buggy, and he did some shopping. Then we drove out of town by the Southeast Light, and stopped and visited Clark, the lighthouse keeper, for awhile. After a bit, we headed back to L. David's house, down Mitchell Lane, and got the horse unhitched and put away in the barn. By then it was just about turning dark.

"Miss Ida was there in the house, and she invited me in for some milk and cookies. Didn't have to do much persuading! In I went, and pretty soon, I was sitting at their table with a great big molasses cookie in my hand and some milk in front of me.

"As we were sitting and talking, I heard this noise outside — a bumpety-bump-bump-bump, like something running down the hill to their house. Something big, it sounded like. It got louder, and seemed to stop short, right at the door of the house. Then again, bumpety-bump-bump-bump, getting louder and louder, right up to the door, real loud – then it stopped. This happened about three times. Couldn't have been the horse in the barn — this thing, whatever it was, was coming from a good distance!

"I was looking all around by this time, and I must have looked pretty nervous. I was just a young boy. And L. David saw me looking; he put a hand on my shoulder, and he said, 'Don't you worry, Arthur — it's never come in here yet!'

"And just about then, Miss Ida told me, 'You'd better start along home now, Arthur, so your mother won't be worried about you.'

"Well, I'll tell you, I sure didn't want to go out there right then, after hearing that noise coming down the hill! But I knew I should start for home, so I did.

"Now, the old-timers on the Island always used to tell stories of a headless white ox that was supposed to be roaming around Mitchell Lane and those parts.

"There was another story the old-timers told about that area, too. Right at Franklin's Corner on Lakeside Drive, where the new road was put in that goes up to the dome house, there used to be a big black rock. Everyone called it Devil's Rock, and told stories about hearing something running around it at night, dragging chains. The rock's underground now. They covered right over it when they put that road in. But in those days, none of us kids ever went by Devil's Rock after dark, and we went by it pretty fast during the day. We didn't like to be around there at all!

"I remembered those stories, coming home that evening, after what I'd heard down at the Spragues' house. I remembered them, and I'll tell you, I made tracks for home like you wouldn't believe, all the way up the lane and back to our house! I sure didn't want to meet up with any headless white ox, or the Devil, or anything else that night!"

Arthur Francis Rose was born in the little white house on Fresh Pond on November 16, 1921, to Bridget Carroll and Ezra Arthur Rose. His mother was Irish and his father was a direct descendant of Tormut Rose, one of the 16 settlers who came to the Island from Massachusetts and settled here in 1661.

Arthur attended the one-room Center School and went to high school in the building that is now the Block Island Health and General Store. He then went to work for the power company as a pole climber. "There was no bucket," he observed. "Once you got up there, it was two hands for the company, and the belt was for you."

He also drove a truck for Giles Dunn, a Rhode Island state senator who owned two fish markets, one at Payne's Dock and one at Old Harbor. Arthur met Eleanor Ruth Ballard on Block Island in the early 1940s, and the two started keeping company. Eleanor had arrived here in 1934 at age 18 to work for her uncle, Henry Ballard. Henry and his wife, Alice, owned Ballard's Inn at Old Harbor.

When the U.S. entered World War II, in 1941, Arthur joined the army. He became a staff sergeant and served in the invasion of Europe, crossing the continent to Salzburg. He returned to Block Island in 1945. Seven years later, on September 29, 1952, he and Eleanor Ballard were married.

The couple's first home on Block Island was at Sands Farm, one of several properties that Arthur took care of. The owner, Colonel Hart, converted a former cow barn to a cottage for the young couple. Sands Farm was later sold to Jean Beck, and the main house became known as the Beck House. The property is now known as Lynn's Way.

The Roses also lived for 18 years in the red house at Red Gate Farm, where they kept cows, horses, chickens, ducks and pigs. The property was owned by Richard Dodge, nicknamed "Dead Eye Dick." It was Dodge who built the restaurant of that name at New Harbor.

Throughout the years, Eleanor and Arthur held a variety of jobs. Eleanor wallpapered and painted, repaired automobiles and worked as cashier at the market. She papered the walls of the huge Ocean View Hotel by herself, and her wallpaper was in place when the hotel burned in 1966.

Arthur was town police chief for 13 years, fire chief for 10, and for many years the Island's state game warden. An electrician by trade, he served as the town electrical inspector.

Arthur celebrates his 84th birthday in November 2005. Eleanor passed away in July 2005.

"In the old days," summarized Arthur, "we took on a lot of jobs to try to help people, especially the old people."

Arthur's knowledge of the Island is encyclopedic. He knows its geography, houses, roads, byways, harbors and ponds, and he can take even long-time Island residents down roads they've never seen before. While his companions may become completely disoriented during one of these ventures, Arthur never is; he knows exactly where he is, and exactly which roads lead – or do not lead, or no longer lead — out.

What lurked in the attic?

"I T WAS THE END OF THE SUMMER IN 1971," Rally began, recounting another of his ghostly encounters at the Beck House, just up the road from us. "It was about ten o'clock in the morning. Diana and I had packed up the car with all the suitcases, pets, and everything else we'd brought with us. We were ready to leave for the boat, but we couldn't find the cat! It was a little orange cat, named Marmalade.

"We looked everywhere, on all three floors of that house, in the basement, in every corner, and we still couldn't find Marmalade.

"On the second floor of the house, in the oldest section at the rear, there was a bedroom. Jean Beck's youngest son, Corky, had stayed there when he lived in the house. Above that bedroom was a little attic, separated from every other room. When the house was built, that attic was put on as a death room. In the old days, when people died during the winter, their corpses were put in cold storage in the death room until spring. When the ground softened, they could be buried.

"There was a little narrow staircase that went up to that attic, and the staircase was behind a door that was always shut tight. I didn't see how the cat could have gotten up there, but you never know with cats. It was the only place I could think of where we hadn't looked, so I opened the door to the attic and started up the stairs.

"I went about halfway up, and looked — and when I looked into that attic, I saw a face, with a sort of hairy-looking, indistinct outline. And that face had a pair of burning, red eyes in it, and it was coming toward me! It scared the hell out of me! The hairs on the back of my neck went right up, and I backed out of there fast!"

Rally, I should add here, is a big, rugged man. He worked out regularly in his younger years, served as a sergeant in the military police in Naples, Italy, at the end of the Second World War, and stays fit and active. He is physically very strong, and has a grip and handshake that often surprise younger men. He is not afraid of much, as a rule.

"I yelled for Diana to bring me a flashlight," Rally continued. "She did, and I went back up the attic stairs with the light. The cat, meantime, had been found someplace else in the house.

"When I took that flashlight and shone it all over the attic, there was nothing there. Diana and I both looked in every corner, and it was empty. It was a small, tight room, with no windows, no vents, no doors, no cracks, no nothing — just a room. There was no way that anything, like an owl or an animal, could have gotten in or out.

"But those red eyes were there the first time I went up those stairs! I'll never forget them, and I'll never forget how scary they were!"

"You saw the red eyes too?" asked Kurt Tonner incredulously, when he overheard Rally telling this story at a party one evening. *"I saw the red eyes!"*

Kurt is a chef and caterer who now lives on Beacon Hill. For seven summers, after Rally and Diana had built their own house and were no longer staying at the old farm, Kurt and his wife, Erica, and their three children, lived in the Beck House from mid-June to September.

"I was always a disbeliever," said Kurt, "even though I'd heard lots of stories about that house.

"One night, the summer of 1979 I think it was, we had guests in the house, and I was telling them about the death room, and why it was called that. I'd never been up to that particular attic, though from time to time I'd opened the door and thrown a box up to get it out of the way. Occasionally, too, I used the stairs as shelves. I'd never heard any stories about the room, other than that it was used to store bodies in the winter.

"One of the guests challenged me to take them all upstairs and show them this death room, so up we went. I opened the door to the stairs, and went up maybe three or four steps. Just as I got in sight of the attic, I looked up and saw a pair of almond-shaped, piercing, fiery red eyes, staring down at me! I didn't stay to see anything else, I just got out of there fast — those eyes were scary!

"The next day, I got my courage up and went back up the stairs to the attic to look for windows that might have had reflections in them. As I said, I was a disbeliever, and always tried to find some rational explanation for things that happened. But that room is just a closed, single room with no way out or in, no windows or glass, no nothing.

"For years, I just kept my story to myself. I had no idea that anyone else had seen the red eyes."

At least one other person did, though, and that was in the 1960s: during the years that young Corky Beck was growing up, he slept in the rear second-floor bedroom of his mother's house. Corky left the Island in the late 1960s, and when he came back to visit, he refused to sleep in his old room.

"I had enough of that guy with the red eyes," he said, when asked about his reluctance to live in his former bedroom. Corky even had a name for the red-eyed apparition: he called it Argyle, and said that Argyle sometimes came down the attic stairs to visit the room below. As Corky said, and as Rally and Kurt seemed to agree, enough of "that guy with the red eyes" was definitely enough.

28

THE CLOCK LADY, AND OTHER
WEST SIDE TIMEKEEPERS

WHEN MY STORIES ABOUT GHOSTS began to appear in the Island newspaper, several friends told me of a mysterious "Clock Lady" who had been appearing and disappearing over on the Island's west side for some years.

The first of these stories was told to me by "Captain Bob" Cottle. Bob's face had been familiar to me for years, when I lived in the Boston area; he was a successful artist who had a long-running show on Boston's public television channels, teaching children of all ages how to draw along with him. I was a young, married career woman when I first saw his show, but was nevertheless quite taken with this handsome, white-bearded artist who patiently explained the reason for each line that he rendered. I watched his show every so often and drew along with him in a hopeful spirit, undeterred by lack of artistic ability. It never occurred to me that I might meet the mythical-seeming Captain Bob, but when I came to Block Island, there he was, spending summers at his house on Corn Neck Road. Rally had known him for years.

The incident that Bob recounted had taken place about 30 years before, in the 1960s, when he, his late wife, Betty, his mother-in-law, and his son were taking a spin around the Island.

"We were taking a leisurely little Island tour, the four of us, one evening," he told me, "and as we were approaching Cooneymus Road from West Side Road, the headlights picked up a person standing, facing us, on the other side of the road.

"It was a lady, and she was dressed in something long and light and floating, like a white nightgown, and her hair was piled up on top of her head. I slowed down, and as we drew near, we could see that she was pointing, with her right hand, to an alarm clock that she was holding in her left hand. She appeared to be disturbed about something.

"She struck us as a bit odd, and we thought she might be in some sort of distress, so I stopped the car on the southbound side of the road and got out. I turned, and started walking back to where she had been standing.

"She was gone! There was nobody there at all. I looked all around, by the sides of the road, everywhere, but she had simply vanished: no lady, no white gown, anywhere to be seen. My feeling is that if she was a living person, she certainly pulled a fast, quiet disappearing act — there were no sounds of anyone in the bushes, no sign that anyone had been there. But, she had been there just a moment before. All four of us had seen her, and thought her rather strange, and now she was gone. We all felt considerably shaken up by the experience."

Nonagenarian Fred Benson, that avowed non-believer in ghosts, had never seen the Clock Lady himself, but he told me of a woman who had come into his office one summer about five or six years before, in the mid-1980s, and had seemed very agitated.

"Do you know," the lady demanded, "that on Old Mill Road, at dark, a woman shows up carrying a clock?" Fred said that he had not been aware of it, but he added that the story spread, and he began to hear it from other people as well. And, four days after the agitated lady had come into his office, he heard from another source that in a house near the West Side Road end of Old Mill Road, a clockmaker and repairer had once lived. "The woman who came into my office four days before had not known anything about that," he told me.

"Oh, sure," said West Side Road resident and Island native Arthur Rose, weighing in with his own take on the Clock Lady story: "The clockmaker was Jim Lindsay. When I was a boy, my father and I used to walk over and visit him in that house, that would be, oh, about 60 years ago. I loved to go in there, because he had clocks all over the place, ticking away, and at the hour, they'd all strike together. To me, it was an interesting place.

"That lady that Bob Cottle saw," continued Arthur, "was probably just Ed Burt's wife. The Burts rented that same house for awhile, and she was a little strange, but she was alive enough, not a ghost."

Another resident of West Side Road, Elliot Sanford, was quite informative, too.

I had met Elliot on Block Island four years earlier, in 1986, the morning after I had met Rally. I was flying off-Island, on my way to a writing assignment in South Carolina. In the waiting room at the Block Island Airport, and also flying that morning, was a slight, dapper man with a halo of white hair, an aquiline nose, and gentle laugh lines around his very piercing, observant eyes. We were seated next to each other in the small, single-engine plane, behind two young men who kept leaning forward and peering around with apprehensive looks on their faces as the plane buzzed down the runway, took off, and headed over the water to Westerly. "Nervous chaps," Elliot murmured to me with the merest hint of a smile lurking around his mouth as he nodded toward the two. He quietly folded his slim hands on his lap and settled in for the 15-minute flight.

I was fortunate enough to become further acquainted with Elliot, once I moved to the Island. He and I were both members of the Block Island Writers' Workshop, a group of writers who met for regular discussions, shared their writings, and from time to time published small books of their collected works. Elliot, I learned, had been hired in 1926, at age 24, by Harry Houdini, as Houdini's personal secretary. Houdini died shortly thereafter, and it became Elliot's job to oversee the disposition of the famous magician's estate. After two decades of other career moves, Elliot married his fiancée, Mary Lou, in 1947. The couple raised two daughters, traveled, and in 1967 built their retirement home on Block Island. When I met Elliot, in 1986, he was 84 years old, happily living year round on the west side with Mary Lou. He was an accomplished pianist and writer, had a wonderfully dry sense of humor, and took pride in the couple's ten great-grandchildren.

"About 30 years ago, which is when Bob Cottle saw the Clock Lady," Elliot told me that day in 1990, when we were discussing that particular apparition, "three friends of ours, ladies who had all been to nursing school together, owned a house next door to Rustic Rides on West Side Road.

"These ladies said that the Clock Lady was a real person, a lady who was a little fey, and had a 'thing' about time. Apparently, she made a habit of wandering around at night with a clock. They didn't know who she was, though.

"And by the way," added Elliot, who was an avowed skeptic when it came to ghosts, "if you start hearing old timers' stories about 'dancing lights' here and there on the Island, the explanation is simple: in the old days, people used to go out at night in a horse and buggy, and they'd tie a light to the wagon to act as a sort of headlight and running light. The light would jiggle around with the movement of the wagon, and, being fairly high off the ground, would reflect in any windows that caught it, from any angle, and it would look like dancing lights. So, that's what those stories are all about!"

Elliot did, however, call back two minutes later with a "clock story," an experience that he and Mary Lou had had at their home on West Side Road. "We have a grandfather clock in our house, we've had it for years," he told me. "And for years, both the striker and the chime have been broken. The 'boing' didn't work, and neither did the 'boing-boing-boing-boing,' if you know what I mean. It didn't work because, several years ago, the thing started striking like crazy at 2:00 one morning, and wouldn't stop — so, to shut it up, we took the weights out and just let it tick quietly in its corner for five years.

"But this year, on January 19, the night before Mary Lou's 75th birthday, that clock started chiming again, in its regular pattern, just as it had years before. So that's our only experience with clocks — but it was a bit eerie."

High Street resident Gaye Voskamp had her own twist on the Clock Lady story. A fellow writer in the Workshop, Gaye has never discounted the existence of ghosts or other paranormal phenomena. A goddaughter of Lester Dodge, who upon his death bequeathed funds to build the Island Free Library, Gaye spent her first 38 summers on the Island and fell in love with it. She moved here in the 1970s with her two sons, Peter and John, to live year round in the High Street house that had belonged to her mother. Gaye has since moved to Narragansett, just across the water. Her former High Street house is now the Island headquarters of The Nature Conservancy.

The day we were discussing the Clock Lady, Gaye told me of an Island tour that she and her friend, Steve Mitchell, had conducted for friends: "One summer day, about 1981, Steve and I were driving some mainland friends around the Island. This was their first visit, and we wanted to give them a little tour before we all went to the beach.

"As we were coming around near Southwest Point, Steve pulled onto Cooneymus Road so we could show our friends 'Westward Ho,' the old lifeboat station. Suddenly, Steve pulled over, stopped the car, and got out, with the engine running.

"'I saw something in the road,' he said, and walked toward the back of the car.

"I tried to think of some interesting tidbit that I could tell our friends about Cooneymus Road, and I remembered Bob Cottle telling me about the Clock Lady that he'd seen about 20 years earlier. So I told them Bob's story, and added that lots of people on the Island had reacted to it with, 'Oh, you saw the Clock Lady, too! Lots of people see her!' My friends seemed entertained, but skeptical.

"Just then, Steve came back to the car with the thing he'd seen in the road. He said disgustedly, 'I thought maybe it was something interesting, but it was just this old clock!' and he put it in the car.

"We were all quiet — dead silent would be a better way to put it. It seemed a weird coincidence that I'd thought of telling them that story just as Steve had seen a clock, of all things, lying in the road.

"We took the clock home; Steve thought maybe he could fix it, even though the crystal was shattered and the clock appeared to be pretty well banged up. It was hopelessly broken, though, and not running. The alarm hand had been set at 5:30, and the time on the clock face was 12:15 — the exact time Steve had found it lying in the road. We gave up on fixing it and set it on the mantle.

"We never went to the beach that day, because a storm came up. It turned out to be a hailstorm, the only one I've ever experienced on Block Island, and it really raged! And in the middle of that storm, as we were all sitting around the kitchen table, that alarm clock bell went off, at exactly 5:30! It spooked all of us.

"The next day, Steve and I put the clock in the car and drove back to Cooneymus Road. We left it there, behind a stone wall, well hidden — it seemed a scary and unpredictable little thing to us. And as far as we know, it's still there."

THE OFF THE WALL PICTURE

"EARLY ONE EVENING, DURING ONE of the summers that Diana and I were staying at the Beck House — I think it must have been about 1969 — we went out for about an hour, down High Street, to visit Gaye Voskamp," Rally told me.

"Those were the years when I was working at my family's marina at Port Edgewood, in Cranston, and there was a kid from the marina out visiting us, who'd never been to the Island before. He was about 16, and his name was Jimmy. That evening, when we went out to visit Gaye, our daughter Lisa, who was just a little girl, was upstairs sleeping, and Jimmy was down in the living room watching TV.

"When we got back from our visit, it was still early — about 7:00 — but when we came into the living room, we saw Jimmy sitting in a chair with a blanket over his head. He seemed nervous, and he was some glad to see us back again!

"'What's the matter, Jimmy?' I asked him.

"He pointed to the opposite side of the room from where he was sitting, toward the wall where the couch was. 'The picture came off the wall!' he told us. He sounded frightened and his eyes got big and round.

"We looked. On that wall, for years, there had been a picture of gondolas in Venice, a large painting in a gilded frame — but the picture wasn't there.

"'What do you mean? Did you take the picture down, Jimmy?' I asked him.

"'The picture came off the wall by itself, and it went behind the couch!' he told me.

"Diana and I went over and looked behind the couch, and sure enough, there was the picture, resting against the wall.

"'It went behind the couch — all by itself,' Jimmy told me again.

"Now, that picture was huge, as long as the couch. The frame was very heavy and ornate, and it stood out about three inches from the picture itself.

"The couch was heavy, too, and it fit right up tight against that wall, without any space between the top of the couch and the wall. There's no way that picture could have just gone behind the couch — but it was there!

"And another thing: the picture had been suspended by several pieces of strong piano wire, and it had been hanging on three big spikes that had been driven into the wall at a steep angle.

"We moved the couch; it took all three of us to do it. We looked at the back of the picture. Not one of those wires on the picture had been broken; and the three spikes were still angled into the wall, just the way they'd been driven in. That picture didn't just fall down — the house would have had to be turned upside down, for that to happen.

"But according to Jimmy, that picture had just come off the wall, quickly and quietly, and gone behind the couch. That was all — but that was enough. He was some scared, and he never came back to the Island again!"

OF MOVING FURNITURE AND OVERHEAD STEPS

FORMER HIGH STREET RESIDENT Gaye Voskamp is a believer in ghosts. Perhaps, for that reason, ghosts have sought her out. Cynics might suggest, of course, that those who believe in ghosts see and hear supernatural phenomena because they want to believe in them — or that, for the same reason, believers interpret everyday occurrences as supernatural ones. Nevertheless, the ghosts described here — if that is what they are — have made themselves known to others as well as to Gaye.

When Gaye told me this story, she was living in the High Street house that had belonged to her mother. "Late one night, about 11:00," Gaye told me, "I was in my house with my two sons, my brother, and my sister-in-law. This was about 1976. My son John and I were downstairs, and everyone else was upstairs, asleep.

"All of a sudden, John and I heard the most awful racket — it sounded as if someone was dragging heavy furniture, and lots of it, across the floor of my bedroom, which was directly above us. The noise went on for awhile, then stopped.

"We went upstairs to see what was going on, but everyone was sound asleep, and there was nobody in my bedroom. It couldn't have been a tree, because there aren't any outside my bedroom window, and anyway, it didn't sound like that — it was something being dragged across the floor.

"John and I mentioned it at breakfast the next morning, and asked if anyone else had heard the noise, but no one else had been up, and no one had heard anything.

"Another time, a friend of ours, Henry Brown, stayed with us in the house. He was in the house alone for awhile. When the rest of us returned, I mentioned to him, offhandedly, that my son and I had heard noises upstairs before, when we were sure that nobody was up there.

"'Like furniture being moved?' he asked. 'I heard that while you were gone — sounded like a lot of stuff scraping across the floor of your bedroom. I went up and checked, but the room was empty.'"

Gaye also told me that about six years before my conversation with her took place, in 1984, Rally had been taking care of her cat while she was away on vacation. He went to her house twice a day to let the cat in and out, and make sure she had food and water. One morning, about 9:00, Rally was in Gaye's kitchen feeding the cat, when the telephone rang. He answered it — it was Gaye, calling for him and thinking she might be able to catch him while he was there. As they were talking, Rally heard some noises upstairs.

"Gaye," he said, "it sounds as though there's someone upstairs in your

bedroom, moving furniture around! Hang on, I'll go check it out —
sounds as if somebody's up there!"

"Steve and I locked the bedroom door before we left," Gaye told him,
"and there was no one in it when we did!"

Nevertheless, Rally went upstairs to have a look. As he reached the top
of the stairs, the noise stopped. The door to the room was indeed
locked, just as Gaye had left it, with no key in sight. Rally banged on
the bedroom door, and called, and listened for awhile, but there was
just the silence of an empty room.

"No one here," he reported to Gaye over the phone, "but I know I just
heard those noises!"

"Well, you aren't the only one," replied Gaye.

Gaye told me this story in 1990 — and as far as she knew, her furni-
ture-arranging ghost still lurked on the second floor, from time to time.
Gaye's son Peter, now managing editor of *The Block Island Times*, supplied a further detail about his mother's former home: "A series of
informal Ouija board sessions reportedly revealed that the house, built
in the mid-late 19th century, had once been a rooming house. And,
according to information gleaned from the Ouija board, a fellow
named 'Clarence Toppe' fell asleep in bed with a lit cigarette and did-
n't survive. None of this lore was confirmed, however."

In the spring of 2004, I checked in with Scott Comings, the Block Island
Landscapes Director for The Nature Conservancy. Gaye Voskamp's
former house is now The Nature Conservancy's Block Island office.

Scott is a lanky man in his 30's, who, despite his easy drawl and
relaxed manner, is in constant motion. I was surprised to find him at
his desk when I called his office; he is far more likely to be found in
field, forest or pond, instructing Block Island's school children on
birds, beetles, bees and sundry other creatures that cross the students'
paths of study or travel. A field ornithologist and master bird bander,
Comings graduated from Earlham College with a major in biology
and minor in education, then spent 4-1/2 years working at internships
in field ornithology under the auspices of Brown University, the
Smithsonian Institute Migratory Bird Center, Louisiana State
University, and the University of California at Davis. Field studies of
some 1400 species of birds a year took Scott to the Louisiana bayous,
Panama, and Guatemala, but his heart and his chosen home base are
on Block Island. When the job with the Block Island office of The
Nature Conservancy was formed, through funding by Island resident
Josephine Merck, Comings applied. He began his work here in March
1997.

"Scott, I'm working on my ghost stories," I told him. "Have you, uh,
ever had any strange experiences at your office on High Street?" I was
a bit hesitant to ask this busy scientist such a frivolous-sounding ques-

tion.

"Oh, sure!" he responded. "I've heard footsteps upstairs, above my office, early in the morning; I guess that was four or five years ago. From what I understand, the room upstairs is where the Voskamps used to hear things from time to time."

"That was where the moving furniture was," I told him.

"Yeah, that's right," he replied, "but what I heard was heavy steps, like a man's footsteps, very loud and very distinct. It was pretty bizarre, and I knew for a fact that there was no one else in the house."

Scott continued, "I've also come in a couple of mornings, early, and all the windows on the north side and east side of the house have been open. That's happened twice. It was in the middle of winter, and all the windows had all been closed the evening before, when we left for the day. Again, pretty bizarre.

"And I believe that one of the scientists we had staying here also saw something dart out of that room upstairs, above my office, and go into another room, but that's all I remember him telling me.

"My dog won't go upstairs in this house," concluded Scott, of his chocolate Labrador, Jake. "I've heard that they're sensitive to the supernatural."

A few months later, in the fall of 2004, Comings recounted a further anecdote to Peter Voskamp, who passed it along to me: "In the early fall of 2004, Comings and Conservancy colleague Charlotte Herring were surprised to find that the door to the room upstairs, the source of many an odd noise, was shut.

"Not only was it shut, but it was locked. And, what's more, it was bolted, from the inside.

"Comings had to climb up a ladder and through a window to open up the room once more.

"Clarence must have been feeling restless."

WHAT THE DOG SAW

OR 16 YEARS, Rally had a dog named King, a 130-pound, long-haired German shepherd — fearful-looking, but, in Rally's words, "The gentlest dog you'd ever want to see." King had died the year before I came to Block Island, so unfortunately I never knew him.

King lived with Rally and Diana during the years they spent summers in the Beck House. King, in fact, grew up in the old farmhouse. In later years, after the couple had built their own house and were no longer living in the old house during summers, Rally looked after the place for his brother-in-law, John Beck, who had inherited it. King, Rally's constant companion in those days, invariably accompanied him to the Beck House on these occasions.

"One time," Rally recalled, "I had to get into the house for some reason — to fix something, or get something that was in there. I no longer had a key; I had to go in through one of the dining room windows. King followed me through the window.

"We went through the dining room into the front hall. I started to walk to the right of the staircase, through the narrow section of hall that led toward the kitchen at the rear of the house.

"All of a sudden, King stopped. He wouldn't go any farther. I was in that section of the hallway next to the staircase, but King would not follow me there. He wouldn't go through that particular part of the hall for anything.

"From that time on, whenever I was in the house, King would follow me in but he'd never go through that hallway. I used to take friends in with me, just to show them how King was acting. I'd have him on a leash, and I'd pull at the leash, but he'd just dig his feet in and snarl at me — and he was a dog who would *never* think of hurting me or anyone else in the family, or anyone who was our friend.

"The house was laid out so people could walk to the back section through that front hall; through the living room to the right of the front entrance; or through the dining room to the left of the front entrance. It was a traditional design.

"King would not hesitate to go around through the back of the house the other way, through the living room, and enter the front hall from the dining room. But, since that one day he had gone into the house with me, he would never go through the side part of the hall leading back to the kitchen. It was as though he could see something there that was stopping him, something we couldn't see.

"If we could coax him to go upstairs with us, he would slink close to the wall, as far away from that hallway as he could get, then go up the stairs as fast as he could go.

"After we got upstairs, there were certain rooms that King would avoid. And there were other rooms that he would go into on one side only, and then he'd stop short, turn around, and go out again, being very careful to go out exactly the same way he came in — there were certain parts of some rooms that he just would not set foot in.

"On these occasions, when the group of us left the house, King would rush out the door after us. He always waited until we were all out of the house, and he'd come out last, as if he was protecting us. He always had to relieve himself immediately, first thing as soon as he came out, as though he'd been nervous about something.

"There are stories about things happening in that hall, but not necessarily in that particular part of it. A woman who said she was psychic visited the house once, and saw a vision of a baby either falling or being dropped from the upstairs to the hall below. There is also a story about a child dying in the house and being buried under an apple tree out back, but that's as much as I know about that.

"One of the previous owners of the house was Colonel Hart, a retired Army colonel. He had a heart attack and collapsed in the hallway, but that was upstairs, not the downstairs hall."

Rally added that he was in the house alone once, coming down the stairs to the front hall, and felt something push from behind, like a person giving him a shove — but no one was there.

"My feeling about that house is that it's a doorway, a connection with another world," he once told me.

The clock that wasn't

"ONE OF THE ODDEST EXPERIENCES I HAD IN THE BECK HOUSE," Rally told me, "was when I was walking through it with an employee of mine named Gary. We'd walked through the whole house and were up on the third floor, talking, when Gary suddenly stopped. 'I hear a clock striking!' he said. "Listen!'

"We both listened and I heard it too, plain as day and loud as Big Ben. It sounded like a big grandfather clock, down in the front hall, and the noise seemed to roll right up the stairs, it was that loud and that distinct. After awhile, it stopped.

"'There's no clock anywhere in this house,' I said. I knew there wasn't. The house had just been shut down for the winter, and there was no electricity, no running water, nothing that would have made any noise at all. And I'd been through the whole place thoroughly, many times, and knew there was no clock.

"But just to satisfy ourselves, we searched through every floor, every corner, and every closet in that house, opening every single door. We even looked in the basement. We thought maybe someone had left a clock in a closet some place, although what we heard had certainly sounded like a big grandfather clock down in the front hall. There was not a clock to be found anywhere — but we'd both heard it striking!"

NIGHT VISITORS AT SANDS FARM

PEOPLE WHO HAVE STAYED IN THE BECK HOUSE, at the old Sands Farm, have reported hearing footsteps and voices during nights, when no one else was there. Other people have seen evening visitors of various sorts.

Kurt and Erica Tonner, who lived at the Beck House for seven summers before buying their house on Beacon Hill, sometimes heard footsteps on the stairs and in the hallway when they knew they were the only ones in the house, and neither one of them happened to be where the footsteps were.

On another occasion, owner Evelyn Beck was staying there overnight with a houseguest. Evelyn, or Evvie, as all in the family know her, is the wife of the late John Beck, who had inherited the house from his mother. John, sadly, perished in an airplane crash in the late 1980s, but these occurrences took place before then, when John and Evvie spent summers at their house.

The night Evvie and her guest were staying at the Beck House, the two women were in separate rooms. During the night, each of them heard voices and steps in the hallway. Each woman assumed that it was the other who was making these sounds. The next morning, the houseguest happened to mention the noises she had heard during the night. Evvie responded that she hadn't been up at all — but had heard the same noises.

Evvie once told me about an experience she had had one night, when she was alone in the house: "I was sleeping in the front northeast bedroom, the one John and I always used, but he wasn't on the Island that night.

"During the night, I woke up and saw a woman sitting at the foot of the bed. She had long hair and long clothing of some sort, and I couldn't feel any weight on the bed where she was sitting. She just sat there and looked at me.

"I'd heard stories from the rest of the family about ghosts in the house, and I'd heard footsteps when there was nobody around, but I'd never seen anything before. I asked her who she was.

"'You know me,' she told me, and I couldn't tell whether she then said, 'I'm Ginny,' or 'I'm Jeanie.' Then she disappeared.

"There was a Virginia Sands who once lived in that house; and of course my mother-in-law's name was Jean Beck. But I'll never know exactly who that woman was who sat on my bed, because she just vanished."

Another Sands Farm visitor was seen by John Fournier. John is a carpenter by trade, as well as a consummately patient wildlife photographer who will spend hours in a homemade bird blind to take amazing telephoto pictures of Island birds in the wild, nesting and feeding their young. He is also a bow hunter of deer, and has dedicated much time and effort to clearing a bow hunting maze and practice area to hone his skills. A reflective and quiet man who is accustomed to his own company and was attracted to Block Island because of his love of nature, John spent several weeks one summer, during the 1970s, living in the Beck House. He stayed in the front northwest bedroom on the second floor.

"I lived at Beck Farm the last part of the summer, into the early fall," he told me in the spring of 2004. I had called him, requesting a retelling of the story that he had told me years before, when I had neither pen nor paper with me.

John continued, "No one had ever mentioned ghosts or anything to me, no one! I didn't know of anything unusual ever happening in that house. My dog, a Labrador retriever, would never go upstairs with me when I was staying there, and I thought that was odd. I kept trying to get him to go up at night, but he just wouldn't, so I used to leave him downstairs.

"One night, in the early fall, I came home, went up to my room, and went to bed. In my room, there was a grate in the floor, an air register that opened to the living room below. As I was lying in bed, I happened to look over toward the grate, and there seemed to be something moving over it, dust or something, like when you see dust moving in the sunlight. But there was no sunlight. It was dark. I thought there might be light coming up through the register from the room below. I looked again, and the dust seemed to have a human form, but with no definition to it.

"I looked away from the register, and then I saw the form standing at the foot of my bed. It was tall, and seemed to have a human form. I could see it was the shape of a woman with her hair in a bun, an older woman, but with no definition to her features. She just stood beside the bed and looked at me, and didn't say or do anything.

"After awhile, I rolled over and went to sleep.

"There were quite a few people living in the house at the time, about six or eight of us. A couple of days later, we were all sitting around downstairs. Someone mentioned that something odd had happened to him that same night. As it turned out, once we started talking, everyone had a strange circumstance or something that had happened that night.

"Two girls were really scared. They were staying in the bedroom at the rear of the second floor, with its own bathroom and the "death room" above. They said they saw someone or something go into their bathroom that night. They never heard anything; whatever it was, it made no noise, but they saw it.

"Someone else, one of the guys, heard a lot of laughing and talking during the night, and thought there was a party outside on the front porch. He was kind of ticked off, because he thought he was missing out on it! He got up twice to check it out, but there was nothing happening and no one there.

"Most of us weren't afraid at all. We wouldn't have said anything about the things we saw or heard if someone else hadn't happened to mention something. My own experience wasn't scary at all, just an odd event.

"I stayed in that room another four weeks, and had no more occurrences of anything strange."

During the early 1990s, two more evening visitors made an appearance at the Beck House.

For quite a few years, members of the staff at Rally's marina, the Block Island Boat Basin, rented rooms for the summer at the old house, which was routinely used to house summer help.

One young man who worked for us was Rob Browne, a high school student from Barrington, Rhode Island. Rob worked at Rally's dock office for several years, docking boats, registering customers in and checking them out, bagging ice and doing painting, carpentry and the myriad other tasks that keep the marina dock running smoothly all summer long for customers and staff alike. Social but not a party-goer, Rob had a ready sense of humor and was well-liked by everyone. He was gregarious and diplomatic with customers; when alone, he loved saltwater fishing. Though he liked to sleep late, he was always at work on time in the early morning hours.

Rally often teased staff members about the ghosts at the house. "Have you seen anything up there yet?" he would ask them. Most said no, not really, well maybe, but probably nothing, really. Some said no, nothing at all. Every so often, someone would report an experience out of the ordinary, and one of these was Rob Browne. Rob was normally reticent about discussing personal experiences, particularly strange ones.

Rob had been staying in the rear room on the second-floor, the bedroom in the oldest section of the house with the "death room" attic above it. It was one night at the end of the summer, in early fall, Rob told us, when he woke and felt something strange. "I woke up from a sound sleep, or at least it seemed I was awake. Something had grabbed both of my legs, something very strong, and I couldn't move them at all. Then, it felt as though something was sitting on me. Again, it was something heavy and very strong, but there was nothing there that I could see or hear. Whatever it was had me pinned down, so I couldn't move. It was really terrifying!" Rob struggled, and eventually the thing, whatever it was, went away, and

Rob lived to tell the tale.

Another young man, J.H. Sava, worked at Rally's marina during four of the years that Rob worked there. J.H. was one of several prep school students from New Hampshire who had come to Block Island for the summer to work as dock boys. Tall and athletic, J.H. was a serious skier who entered pre-Olympic competitive events. He was quiet, kept to himself, took care of his health and didn't drink. Like several other members of our dock staff, J.H. rented a summer room at the Beck House.

"You ever see anything strange up at that house?" Rally asked various staff members that summer, as usual.

J.H., who was probably the most quiet, serious and reserved person then in residence at the Beck House, told Rally about an early-evening experience. "Everyone else was out of the house," he said. "I was lying on the couch in the living room, watching TV and relaxing.

"I saw a woman come into the room, from the direction of the front hall. She walked through the living room, toward me; she was dressed in old-fashioned clothes, and her hair was up on her head.

"When she got between the couch and the TV, I could see right through her! She just kept moving through the room, and went through the door that led to the kitchen."

"What did you do, J.H.?" asked Rally, intrigued.

"Nothing — nothing at all!" replied J.H. with great emphasis.

OF GHOSTLY GUESTS AT ADRIAN HOUSE

THE FIRST GUEST HOUSE ON BLOCK ISLAND was that of Alfred Card, who in 1842 opened his house at Old Harbor to boarders and vacationers. His first guests were seven men from Newport, on the Island for a fishing expedition. Known as the Old Adrian, the house eventually came to be called Adrian House. By the 1870s, it was being kept by Charles Willis, and in the 1890s, Adrian House was the property of Nathan Mott. Mott was the father of the influential, civic-minded Lucretia Mott Ball, founder of the Women's Christian Temperance Union (WCTU) on Block Island and wife of Cassius Clay ("C.C.") Ball. C.C. Ball, who had inherited the Ocean View Hotel from his father, Nicholas Ball, kept a general store on the west side of Water Street at Fountain Square. It was he who donated property for the statue of Rebecca at the Well to the WCTU. C.C. Ball's store building housed the post office for many years and was eventually moved across Water Street, where it is now Ernie's Restaurant.

Lucretia Mott Ball inherited the Adrian House from her father. In 1941, when she died at the age of 74, it was bequeathed to the Island's First Baptist Church. High on a hill overlooking the harbor, Adrian House became the church building in 1944, when a fire destroyed the Baptist church on Chapel Street. Eight years later, a church sanctuary was added to the front of Adrian House to create the present Harbor Church.

The rear part of the building, the old Adrian House, is the church's Fellowship Hall. It houses the church kitchen and Sunday School, and is a gathering place for church and community suppers, fairs, and other events. On the second floor of Fellowship Hall are the pastor's office, an apartment that serves as the pastor's residence, a church office, and a caretaker's apartment. The third floor contains a long corridor with a number of rooms. One is used for storage by the Block Island Ecumenical Choir, but the other rooms on this floor remain empty and unused.

"I lived on the second floor of Adrian House from the spring of 1990 to the fall of 1995," Tom Wilkinson told me. Tom, who spent summers on Block Island all his life before moving here in 1989, is a member of the management team of Block Island Resorts, the company that owns the Hotel Manisses and The 1661 Inn, and manages a number of other properties.

Tom continued matter-of-factly, "I had odd experiences there, and so did a number of other people. I lived in the pastor's apartment on the second floor; at the time, Tony Pappas was the pastor, and the Pappases had their own house on Lakeside Drive. Two roommates shared the apartment with me: Jeff Liptak, a bartender at the Hotel

Manisses, and Deb Wall, who worked at the daycare center. Very often, we would hear footsteps above us. They were very distinctly the footsteps of one person, walking across the third floor. We all heard the footsteps from time to time — and we all knew the third floor was empty.

"One night, Jeff and I heard the footsteps and we went up to the third floor with a flashlight to see if there was actually someone up there — but no one was. There's a second set of stairs in the building, leading from the third floor up to an unfinished attic. We got to those stairs and slowly started going up, but we both had a creepy feeling about the stairs and the attic. We both got goose bumps, and decided we didn't want to go up there just then. We went back to the second floor, and we heard no more sounds that night.

"At other times," Tom continued, "We would see images, like reflections, moving through the second floor. Deb, Jeff and I were sitting in the living room of our apartment one evening, just chatting. The television screen was positioned so that it picked up reflections from the hallway outside our door. As we sat there, all three of us saw a shape going down the hall. It was a small image, and it went back and forth in the hallway. There were no features to it, but it was a human shape and resembled a young boy, about 10 years old."

After a moment, Tom told me, "I had another odd experience one day, too. I came home and was going down the hallway, past the open bathroom door. The room was open and empty. The first person I saw was Deb, and I asked her, 'Where's Jeff?'

'In the bathroom,' she said.

'No, it's open and there's no one there,' I told her. I went back through the hall, and this time the bathroom door was closed — and Jeff was in there. I don't know where he came from or how he got there, but the room had been open and empty before, and no one could have gone in without being seen by one of us.

"And then there were the lights," Tom recalled. "We had a ceiling light in the living room of our apartment. One night we were sitting there, and the light came on by itself. No one had touched a switch, it just came on. And then, after awhile, it went off by itself. This happened on two different occasions.

"Sometimes we'd have little after-hours get-togethers at our apartment with other staff members, and some of these events would occur. A couple of the waitresses from the Manisses were so frightened that they wouldn't come back."

Tom added reflectively, "Whatever was there wasn't trying to scare anyone. It was more like an inquisitive presence, a shadowy thing that moved fairly quickly and sometimes hesitated just a split second before moving on. There was never any sound, except of course for the

48

footsteps.

"The last one and a half years that I lived there, there was no activity," he concluded. "But my first four years there, all of the things I've mentioned occurred, more than once. The footsteps were the most frequent; the shadowy images were occasional; and the lights came on and went off by themselves twice.

"Suzanne Wagner was the church secretary at the time, and one day I asked her to ask Tony Pappas about ghosts at Adrian House. He had lived in that apartment for nine years, before the Pappases moved into their house. Suzanne came back and told me that the only ghost Tony wanted to talk about was the Holy Ghost."

Tom laughed, a characteristic sparkle in his dark eyes. "Some time after that, I saw Tony and asked him myself whether he'd had any ghostly experiences when he lived in that apartment.

"'I thought I gave Suzanne a message for you,' he told me.

Concluded Tom, "He never actually gave me a direct answer to my question."

The pastor's apartment is at one end of the second floor hall in Adrian House; at the other end is a smaller apartment, reserved for the church sexton. For five or six years, the sexton at the Harbor Church was Luis Montoya-Velez, a native Colombian who has made Block Island his home while studying classical vocal music to further his dream of singing professionally. Always a hard worker, Luis has been a professional cleaner of homes and businesses and a cheerful, singing employee at the Block Island Grocery deli counter, as well as the Harbor Church sexton — all this, while singing with the Block Island Ecumenical Choir and preparing for numerous solo fundraising concerts to help various Island charitable causes. He studied at an opera school in Florence, Italy for a summer, spent time with his family in Colombia, then returned to Block Island, where he continues tirelessly with his work and his vocal studies.

I saw Luis at the Block Island Fitness Center two days before Christmas in 2004. We were both there for an early morning workout, and I took the opportunity to ask him whether he had ever seen or experienced any ghosts during his tenure at the Harbor Church.

"No," he replied, to my disappointment, then added, "But I used to hear things."

I perked up as I plugged away on the elliptical trainer. "What things?" I asked.

"Laughter! I used to hear people laughing and talking at night, down in the kitchen and in the parlor. Never in the church sanctuary. Every time I heard people, I went downstairs — in the summer, especially, you don't know who's around, and I wanted to make sure nobody had come in the church at night. But there was never anyone. This was many times, for five or six years.

"I used to hear things breaking, too," he added.

"Dishes?" I suggested, thinking of the kitchen.

"More like glass," he said. "But there was never anything."

He added a little sheepishly, "Oh, and sometimes at night, it felt as if someone was sitting on my bed. I could feel the bed go down on one side, and it as if someone was there, but there was never anyone. And this was many times.

"But I never felt scared — it was never anything bad," Luis concluded.

"I had lots of ghosts living with me at Adrian House!" exclaimed Mickey Terrana, when I asked him about his residency there. Mickey was sexton at the Harbor Church for six years, following Luis, and lived in the same sexton's apartment.

Mickey grew up in Providence and visited the Island often as a child. In 1996, he decided to find work on the Island — far enough from the mainland for an independent life, but close enough for frequent visits home. He sent resumés to all the Island hotels and received a reply from Lorraine Cyr, at The Surf Hotel. He came to the Island for an interview, and was hired by the Cyr family. Currently, Mickey works for the Town of New Shoreham at the Wastewater Treatment Facility, and is a resident of Connecticut Avenue.

"I moved to Adrian House before Roll Call Dinner one year," Mickey remarked, referring to the Harbor Church's magnificent turkey dinner with all the trimmings, held every October.

"I used to see things every night in my apartment!" he said excitedly, in his characteristically animated style of speaking. "I wouldn't see anything directly — it was always some movement or some image that I could just see out of the corner of my eye. Sometimes I would lie in bed and watch TV, and have the sense that someone was right there looking at me. Other times, I'd see things flying around the room, moving through the air, but it was with peripheral vision. It was like the Indiana Jones movie, when the Ark of the Covenant is opened and the spirits start flying around — it was just like that!" Mickey gestured in the air, his quick hands flying bird-like around his head. "It got to where I put up crucifixes over my doors, and palm leaves, and a picture of Christ, just to make sure the spirits or whatever they were stayed friendly. And I used to talk to them; when I got in at night, I'd call out, "Hi, how are you?" to all the spirits. I was living alone, but I really wasn't alone.

"Another time," he added, "I'd just had a 'dear John' breakup over the phone from a girl I'd been going with. That night, I was really depressed. I was lying in bed, feeling lousy, and I felt the edge of the bed go down — like someone was sitting on it! And I felt a touch on my lower leg — not a grab, just a touch from a hand.

"And then sometimes there were voices. I'd go downstairs and check the building in the middle of the night, and I'd hear a loud voice, shouting at me — no words, just a loud "Uh-h-h-h-h!" Every time I heard that, I'd go upstairs and close my door.

"My grandmother," Mickey concluded, "used to see the reflections of dead people in mirrors. Psychic sensitivity runs in my family — my mother, my sister, we all have it."

Pastor Pat Harrison returned my call promptly, and gave serious attention to my inquiry about any experiences she might have had with ghosts during her residency in the pastor's apartment on the second floor of Adrian House. Now in the third year of her ministry at the Harbor Church, Pat trained and worked as a medical technician at Rhode Island Hospital, earning a Master's degree in Immunology and Microbiology before being called to the ministry. During her years at seminary, she continued her hospital work to finance her education, graduating in 1998.

The Harbor Church is Pat's second full time pastoral position. Her ready sense of humor and her widespread embrace of the larger Block Island community are indicative of a generous turn of mind that misses very little when it comes to the quirks of human nature.

"I've heard steps upstairs on the third floor while I've been in my apartment," she told me, echoing the experiences of Tom Wilkinson when he lived in the same apartment several years before. "When I've heard the footsteps, I've taken a look up there to see what's going on, and there's never been anything there. But any experiences I've had there have not been frightening.

She concluded with conviction, "I believe in a spirit world, another level of life. I believe there are spirits all around us!"

WHEN OLD SPIRITS ROAMED
THE NEW SHOREHAM HOUSE

WHEN I ARRIVED ON BLOCK ISLAND, Bob and Kathy Schleimer owned the New Shoreham House, in Old Harbor. Behind the inn, they ran a bike rental. In the front part of their building, facing the harbor and with a prime location across from the ferry dock, was their gift shop, Esta's. The former Esta's space is now occupied by the clothing store, Wave.

Bob and Kathy came to the Island from Westchester County, New York, where Bob worked for NBC. Kathy had been coming to Block Island since she was a little girl. The Schleimers took a house here one summer, and decided to move here year round. They looked for a business that would support their family, and found that the New Shoreham House and Esta's were for sale.

The couple moved here in February of 1983, with daughters Deirdre and Hilary, to a three-bedroom apartment above Esta's. Later, as their businesses became more and more successful, the Schleimers bought a house at the north end of Corn Neck and took up residence there.

In addition to being savvy business people, the Schleimers were active in the community. Bob served at least two terms as president of the local Chamber of Commerce, and Kathy also served a term as president. Kathy and I both attended an early-morning exercise class conducted in the basement of St. Andrew's Parish Center by librarian Lonni Todd. For a time, Kathy was a fellow first soprano in the Block Island Ecumenical Choir. As parents of two girls, the Schleimers were also involved in school affairs and fundraisers.

Bob and Kathy sold their businesses in the late 1990s and moved to Providence, Rhode Island, where they have a new age store called Esta's Elementals. In the spring of 2004, both were pursuing graduate studies and potential new careers, Bob in teaching and Kathy in psychology and counseling.

It was about 1991 when Bob Schleimer first told me about odd occurrences at the New Shoreham House.

"When we came to live here," Bob began, "our apartment above Esta's could be closed off from the inn by a door. As soon as we moved in, we started renovations in the building, and almost immediately we started to notice some strange things happening.

"We slept on the second floor, and at night, we sometimes heard the sound of furniture being dragged across the third floor, over our bedroom. Whenever we heard the sound, I'd jump out of bed and run upstairs to see what was going on. I was able to be upstairs, in the room above ours, within seconds of the time we would first hear the noises. But, there was never anyone there, and never a sign that anything had been moved.

"At the time, we had two winter tenants living with us. They worked elsewhere during the day, but came back to their rooms at night to sleep. They complained to us on several occasions about the renovations that they thought we were doing at 3:00 a.m. — they said there was so much noise they couldn't sleep some nights, and they wondered why we couldn't renovate during the day. We assured them that we were working on the place only during the daytime, and that the mysterious night noises weren't coming from us.

"We continued our renovations — during the day, never at night. At that time, our daughter Hilary was about two years old. We noticed several times, when we were working up on the third floor at one end of the building, that she would be down at the other end of the hallway, laughing and talking and carrying on a conversation. When we went to her and asked her who she was talking to, she'd say, 'My friend.'

"That's nice — who's your friend, Hilary?' we'd ask.

"'This little girl,' she'd answer, and then start looking around, as if the little girl had just been there but had disappeared. 'She was right here,' Hilary would say, continuing to look for the friend.

"'Okay,' we'd say, and go back to our work. And then, a few minutes later, we'd hear her talking and laughing with her friend again. This happened several times, and although we never saw the friend, we always got exactly the same reaction from Hilary.

"We had a dog at the time, and we noticed that our dog would never go up to the third floor. He'd dig in his heels, and absolutely refuse to go up the stairs. We could pick him up and carry him to the third floor, but once he was there, he'd put his tail between his legs, and cringe around, and race downstairs again as soon as he could. He definitely did not like that third floor.

"During the summer of 1983, we noticed more and more strange occurrences. Doors would slam by themselves. The furniture-moving sounds continued at night. Objects would drop off tables, without anyone touching them or even being near them. At the time, we explained it all away by saying it was vibrations, or the building settling.

"Then, Thanksgiving weekend of that year, we had a lady from Philadelphia staying with us. She stayed just one night, in the room that is now Room 5, and the next morning she came to us and said that she had to leave the Island. She gave no explanation, but she looked pale and peaked, and her eyes were glazed. I decided that if she had a medical problem of some sort, it was her decision to either stay and seek treatment here or leave, as she suggested, so I told her we were sorry to lose her, but if she felt she had to leave, then she should. The sequel to that particular story came two years later — I'll get back to it in a few minutes.

"Striped bass season was upon us, and fishermen stayed with us from time to time. One, in particular, was a very rugged young man in his twenties. The morning after his first night at the inn, I went in to fix his breakfast, and found him sleeping in the sitting room instead of in his bedroom.

"He woke up when I came in, and asked me if something was wrong with the building. He said that he had been out the night before, surf casting until about 3:00 a.m. By that time, he felt pretty cold and wet, and decided to come inside. He left his waders outside and came up to his room on the third floor. He said that his bedroom was comfortably hot after the cold ocean, and he took off his clothes and lay down on the bed.

"He said that when he lay down, the bed started to shake violently, coming up off the floor and slamming down again. Then he noticed a foul, sulphurous odor. He said that the air in the room became misty, and the room got cold, so cold he could see his breath. He said that the mist seemed to be forming into a figure. He didn't want to stick around to see any more. He used every ounce of strength he had to jump out of bed, and he ran to the sitting room.

"My unspoken reaction at the time was that he'd had a vivid night-mare. But, over the next several months, on into summer, we had a number of guests who would come to us and tell us the same story that the young fisherman had told me. These people had the same experiences of the moving bed, the sulphurous smell, the sudden temperature change, and the mist in the room. These were people who were from different parts of the country and had no particular connection with each other, yet they all reported the same phenomena.

"We became concerned when Hilary began to wake up screaming in the middle of the night. Hilary slept in what is now Room 2, and when she screamed at night, of course we got up. Sometimes we'd find her sleepwalking, with her eyes wide open. One night, we found her standing at the window in her room, looking out, with her hands pressed against the windowpane. She was sound asleep. Other times, we would find her under her bed or under the furniture in the hall or the living room, always screaming, always with her eyes wide open. We decided to let her sleep with us for awhile instead of in her room, and when we did, she slept soundly through the night.

"More things started to happen after that. One day, during the summer of 1984, I was downstairs in the store, on the side where we have the boutique. There was a circular metal t-shirt rack on the floor, full of t-shirts and fairly heavy — a good-sized display. A woman came in and was looking at the shirts, and all of a sudden, the rack went up in the air, slipped upside down, and came down over her head; she was in the middle of the rack and in the middle of a lot of t-shirts. I was worried about her, of course, and went to help her up. She was fine, but her eyes were as big and round as doughnuts. 'Did you see that?' she gasped. And then she just ran out of the store as fast as she could go, and never came back.

"One night, too, about that time, I woke up in the middle of the night and felt a presence of some sort in our bedroom. I woke Kathy and told her, but she went back to sleep. At that time, we had a large wreath on the wall over the head of our bed. Just as Kathy was going back to sleep, that wreath came off the wall, traveled through the air the full length of our bed, and landed on the floor at the foot of the bed.

"After that, the spirits or whatever they were started to harass us. We had, in our bedroom, a Victorian shelf, with a mirror attached to it, that hung on the wall. On the shelf, Kathy had a collection of perfume bottles. One night, when we were in the living room, we heard a crash in the bedroom. When we went in, the shelf and the bottles were lying on the floor, eight feet across the room from the place on the wall where they had been hanging. The whole piece, and all the bottles, were smashed to smithereens.

"Kathy's mother came to visit us not long after. We hadn't mentioned anything to her, or to any of the family, about the strange occurrences at the New Shoreham House. Kathy's mother stayed in one of the rooms at the inn, and at night when she was ready to go to bed, she would go to her room, close and lock the door, and get into bed.

"One night she heard a noise, and saw that the door had come open. She got up, locked the door again, and got back into bed. She heard the door rattling, and it came open again, so she got up and locked it again. Again the door rattled and came open, and this time she got up, closed it, locked it and pushed a chair against it so it couldn't come open. Again she heard the door rattling, and she said that she could actually see the door bowing in as something tried to open it. The door finally came open again, and she felt something or someone jump on top of her and pin her down in bed, holding her arms so she couldn't move. She could feel the weight on her chest, but couldn't see anything. She struggled, and finally managed to get up and out of the bed, and come downstairs to where we were. She wouldn't go back in that room.

"Not long after that, our two mothers were visiting us, with a friend of Kathy's. Kathy's birthday was in July, and the friend gave her a Ouija board as a birthday present. Kathy and both of our mothers, the friend, and Deirdre, our older daughter, would sit up late every night playing with this Ouija board. We had a Ouija board down in the store, too, so they borrowed that and played with two of them. The pointers on the boards went crazy! My mother sat with the group, taking short-hand as fast as she could, to see if there was any sense or any message in the letters that the pointers selected.

"The messages from the boards did make sense, and the stories that emerged were amazing. One story told of a sea captain's spirit that was lost, wandering, and looking for his lost dog. That corresponded with one set of comments that we had gotten from certain guests at the inn; they complained of a barking dog somewhere inside the building that kept them awake nights, and a smell like that of a wet dog.

"The Ouija boards seemed to open a window between this world and another. From that time on, something strange would happen every single day. There were breakages, as objects seemed to be falling off tables more than before. One time, a lock mechanism inside a door reversed itself so that the door couldn't be opened from the inside. The guest in that particular room was trapped inside, and had to yell out the window for help. When I took the lock apart, I could see that the lock had turned around inside the door, and there was no way a person could have accomplished that.

"People's belongings were found in odd places, places where they hadn't been left. Things were never actually missing, they were just moved. One day, Kathy was taking a bath in our second-floor bath-room, and I heard her call me. I went into the bathroom, and found every drawer and cabinet open. They had all flown open at once, while she was in her bath.

"By this time, I was getting tired of these events. Guests were starting to be annoyed that their things were moved around, and there were always the same sporadic complaints of strange smells and noises dur-ing the night.

"I had heard that spirits do not like dogs, so one day I went to the upstairs hallway and told the spirits that I was going to get a big, fierce dog and bring it to stay in the building if they didn't stop bothering us. The odd occurrences continued, so I brought my dog inside, the same dog who didn't like to go up on the third floor. I told the spirits, 'Okay, I've brought my dog and he isn't a big mean dog, but I'm going to get another one if you don't leave us alone!'

"The dog stayed in the building for several nights. One afternoon, he was sleeping across the street, lying against the side of the Harborside Inn. At that time, there was no paved sidewalk there; the area next to the building was the same level as the street.

"That afternoon, as the dog was sleeping, a station wagon with a fam-ily of vacationers in it came along, going east on Chapel Street, between our building and the Harborside. The car was going slowly, and the driver appeared to be in control. Suddenly, the car sped up and veered to the side where the dog was sleeping. It hit the dog, stopped suddenly, then backed up and ran back over the dog, then stopped, went forward and hit him again. I say 'it' hit him, because the driver was totally shaken, and said that the car had gone out of control. He couldn't stop it or prevent it from hitting the dog. The driver was immobilized during the incident, and had no idea how it had happened, or even what had happened. His wife was upset, of course, and his children were in the back seat crying. He clearly didn't do it on purpose. The dog's back was broken, and we had to have him put to sleep.

"After that, I spoke again to the spirits that we believed were in the New Shoreham House. I went upstairs, and said, 'Okay, you did my dog in, and you seem determined to harass us. Just let me know what it is you want, so that we can coexist peacefully. I don't want any more trouble. Just give me a sign of some sort, so I'll know what it is you want from me.'

"I was standing in the bathroom on the second floor, the same one where the cupboards and drawers had come open while Kathy had been taking her bath on that other occasion. There was a sliding door on one of the cabinets down near the floor, and all of a sudden it slammed open, to one side, then slammed shut again. I knew there was something in the room with me, and I asked it if it was peaceful. And then I got a message, like an imprint inside my head, that said, 'Get rid of the Ouija boards.'

"I just knew that those boards had to go — so I took them to the landfill. Once the boards were out of the house, the harassment stopped. On a scale of one to ten, with ten being the greatest level of harassment and one the least, we were back at level one. I think the Ouija boards may have triggered the negative events.

"Over the next year or two, we had a lot of guests, and very few of them reported anything unusual happening to them. I noticed that when anything was reported, it was most often something that had happened to a single room occupant, and nine times out of ten, the occupant was female. The experiences that people reported seemed positive or even playful in nature, nothing bad or frightening.

"It was in 1985 that the lady from Philadelphia, the one who had left so suddenly during Thanksgiving weekend in 1983, called back. 'Mr. Schleimer,' she said, 'you probably don't remember me, but I stayed at your inn on Thanksgiving weekend two years ago and had to leave.'

"I told her that I remembered, and she said that the experience she had had in Room 5 at the New Shoreham House in 1983 had changed her whole life. She told me that a mist had come into her room during the night, accompanied by the sulphurous smell and the sudden cold that other guests had experienced. She said that the mist had formed into the image of a little girl, who had communicated with her at some length. As a result of that experience, the woman had gone back home and entered a religious order.

"She came back for Thanksgiving weekend of 1985, and stayed in the same room for the full three days. She seemed happy just to stay in her room, and when she did come out, she had a dazed but very happy and peaceful look on her face.

"Even though most of the supernatural occurrences had stopped, we were still concerned about Hilary. We decided it was time for us to leave the New Shoreham House and live elsewhere on the Island, and that was when we bought our house on Corn Neck.

"There was an incident reported to us by one of our chambermaids, Patty, in 1987. Patty had been sleeping upstairs one night, and in the morning she came to us and told us that during the night, a mist had come into her room, under the door, and had formed into the image of a little girl. The little girl held out her hand and told Patty to hold onto it. Patty did, and said that she had found herself drifting over Block Island with this little girl, who kept telling her, 'You're safe, you're safe.' And, she was conducted safely back to her room.

"Then, in 1988, on Labor Day weekend, a couple from Michigan came to the desk at the inn and asked for a room. We were fully booked except for one last-minute cancellation. Kathy's sister-in-law was handling the reservations, and told the couple that they could have that room. And then the man said the oddest thing. He looked at her, and he said, 'We're connected.' She said she didn't think she knew them from anywhere.

"The couple went to their room. It was Room 2, the room where Hilary had once slept. Immediately, they came back downstairs and said, 'The room is occupied.'

"Kathy's sister-in-law said that it was vacant, but the man looked at her and said, 'No, it's occupied. I think you know what we mean.' They agreed to take the room, but said that they would need some incense. We sold incense in the store, so they bought some and took it to the room with them.

"The next morning, Kathy and I joined this couple for breakfast at the Harborside. Kathy kept looking and looking at the man, and suddenly she said, 'I know your voice.'

"He said, 'I know that you know my voice.'

"It turned out that the man's name was Barrie Konicov, and he made subliminal self-improvement tapes. I had bought one of his tapes at a store on the mainland, but we had no other knowledge of him, nor he of us — except that we were somehow 'connected,' as he said. Barrie said that he had 'received a message' — that is, something had told him, while he was at his home in Michigan, that he must come to Block Island. He had never heard of Block Island, but he looked it up on the map, came with his wife and ended up at our inn.

"Barrie said that there were some spirits in the New Shoreham House who wanted to be freed, so that they could complete their passage into their next existence. He offered to free the spirits for us. We told him fine, go ahead, so he went back into Room 2 to work at freeing the spirits. When he came back out, he told us that one spirit had been that of a sea captain, who was looking for his lost dog. The spirit of the dog was wandering around a lighthouse high on a bluff here on the Island, which of course had to be the Southeast Light, on Mohegan Bluffs. Barrie had been able to bring the two spirits together, and send them on their way. He said another spirit was that of a little girl who was searching for her mother. In that case, he was unable to make the connection between the two spirits.

"Just after that Labor Day weekend, I got a phone call from a man named Alan Bateman, someone I'd known from twenty years ago, but hadn't heard from in the intervening years. Even though I hadn't kept in touch with him, I somehow knew who he was, as soon as I heard his voice. Alan is a yoga instructor in Manhattan, and he told me that he had just been on Block Island over Labor Day weekend, because he had 'gotten a message' that he was to come to Block Island. He'd searched for a place to stay and ended up at the Harborside, and said that he had spent a great deal of time in our store, without being able to explain why he did so. He had been fascinated, he said, by the store and the building, and had felt something drawing him to it.

"I think there are still spirits here, because we still have incidents from time to time in some of the rooms. But, since we stopped using the Ouija boards, as I said, the incidents have been minor, and rather playful — nothing negative.

"Just two weeks ago, a young woman from Brown University was staying here, and couldn't get back into her room after leaving it. She had put the key in the lock, but couldn't get it out again; it had flipped itself upside-down in her hand, and after that it wouldn't move, no matter how hard she pulled and twisted at it. She came up to the Manisses, where we were having dinner, to tell us she was locked out of her room. I gave her a different room, and the next morning I drilled the lock out of the door of her first room. It was another case of a backward lock — the mechanism had turned itself around inside the door, something that would have been impossible for a person to do without taking the door apart."

"Is it possible to see the upstairs?" I asked Bob, as his stories came to an end.

"Of course," he replied, adding that the only room we couldn't see was Room 3, because it was occupied. We went upstairs: he pointed out the bathroom with the slamming cupboard doors; Room 2, where Hilary once slept; and Room 5, where the lady from Philadelphia had her life-changing experience. "We've had supernatural incidents reported to us concerning several of the rooms," he commented.

He showed me the staircase to the third floor, which his dog had always refused to climb. We went up, and he indicated the end of the hall on the third floor, where Hilary's friend, the mysterious "little girl," used to engage Hilary in conversation as Kathy and Bob worked at the opposite end of the hall.

"We've had some incidents in this room," he added, taking out his keys and reaching toward the door of Room 15, the last room at that end of the hallway. Before he could fit the key in the lock — before he even touched the door — the door to Room 15 gave a very distinct rattle, and a little shake, as if from the inside. The room, however, was not occupied — or was it?

Bob looked at me. "Let's go downstairs now," he said quietly. "I really don't think we want to go in there today, after all."

Bob prefaced and ended his tales of the New Shoreham House by offering me an overnight stay there, free of charge, any time I wanted. I never took him up on his generous offer; I was busy working at Rally's marina during the tourist season, and I wouldn't have felt right occupying a room for free that Bob could rent for money. I thought about it a great deal, however. I had never experienced a ghost, and wondered if fall would be a good time to do so. I quite liked the thought of flying over the Island with the spirit of a little girl. But one cannot select one's ghostly encounter, and when I considered the stories of foul, sulphurous fumes and spirits that sat on people's chests and pinned them down in their beds, I never quite got around to staying at the New Shoreham House.

JUMPING KEYS AND MIDNIGHT VISITORS

I HAVE SOME ADDITIONAL STORIES about ghostly goings-on at Esta's and the New Shoreham House," volunteered Liz Cowles, who worked for Kathy and Bob Schleimer as manager at Esta's for several years. Now the owner of Distant Shores, a sizeable boutique under the National Hotel, Liz lived at the New Shoreham House during the years she managed Esta's, which then occupied the space at the corner of Water Street and Chapel Street.

"The first odd experience I had at the New Shoreham House took place in the summer of 1984," Liz told me. "I had a room in the upstairs apartment, where the Schleimers were living, and at night I would do my laundry in the New Shoreham House laundry room. The room was downstairs, in what is now the rear section of the boutique side of Esta's. It was a closed-off space, and to get to it, we had to go down the back stairs and through the stock room of Esta's.

"Late one night, some time after 11:00, after the store was closed, I was in the laundry pulling my clothes out of the dryer and I had a distinctly uncomfortable feeling, as if someone was in the room with me. I'm not a skittery kind of person, but the feeling grew, until I just had to leave my clothes in the dryer and get out of there. I knew I wouldn't come back to the laundry room that night, and as I walked through the stock room, I felt as if someone was at my heels the whole way. It was just a feeling, but a very distinct one. The next morning, I told Kathy about it, and said jokingly that the next time I did laundry, I'd have to take Ben, the Schleimers' dog, into the laundry with me for protection. "'Oh, Ben won't go into the laundry,' said Kathy. 'He refuses to enter the room.' From that time on, I wasn't too keen on going into the laundry room, either.

"Some time after that, two of the walls in the laundry room became stock space, as the stock from the adjacent room grew. One day, another girl and I spent a long time checking in a huge t-shirt order. As we checked in the shirts, we stacked them neatly, according to size and style, on the shelves of those two walls in the laundry room. It took us hours, and when we were through, we both left the room.

"A little bit later, the other girl went back into the stock room, and I heard her screaming. I went in to see what was the matter, and found one whole wall of t-shirts dumped all over the floor. It was as if the wall had just tilted, spilled all the t-shirts off their shelves, then righted itself again. No one else had been in the room since the time we had checked in the order, and nothing else had moved. The shelves were still securely fastened to the wall, just as they had been — but every single t-shirt from that one wall was on the floor!

"Funny things seemed to happen in the store at night, too, when no one was there. One year, my sister Stacey worked at Esta's. She was very fussy about the hangers on the clothing displays; she liked them all to face the same way. Every night, before closing, she straightened all those hangers so they faced in the same direction. Now, our schedules were set up so that the last person to close the store at night would be the first one to open in the morning. Several times, after she had arranged the hangers at night, Stacey would open the store in the morning and find some hangers — but not all of them — turned around in the rack. She had been the last to leave the night before, and the first person to arrive in the morning, and nobody had been in the store during the night — but those hangers would be turned wrong, as if someone had done it deliberately!

"I had an odd experience with some of the merchandise, too. I remember that I used to keep the lucite toy bins stocked full, and one of the items I stocked was plastic lobster claw harmonicas. One evening, as I was walking by the bins, one of those lobster claw harmonicas flew out of the bin and hit me in the back of the leg as I walked by. It didn't just fall out, because the bin was stocked far enough below the edge that nothing could fall — and besides, it hit me with too much force to be a fall. It was as if somebody, or something, had thrown it.

"The oddest experience I had in the store, though, was with the cash register keys. This would have been in about 1986. Every night, my routine was the same: I "Z"-ed out the main register in the store, getting the day's total and the entire day's worth of register tape with all the transactions and that final "Z" total at the bottom. Then I bundled the receipts, register tape and cash together, turned off the register and locked it, took out the keys, and went to the second register, clear across the store, to "Z" it out. I kept the keys to both registers on one ring, so I would have them with me at all times.

"One night, I had "Z"-ed out both registers, first the main register and then the second one, following my usual routine. After I'd "Z"-ed out the second register, I reached for my cash register keys, but they weren't where I'd left them. I hadn't moved from the spot where I was standing since I'd "Z"-ed the register, so I knew the keys had to be within arm's reach — but they weren't there. I looked for ten minutes, and I went through the wastebasket, but there were no keys.

"My sister Stacey was working at the jewelry counter, in a different part of the store, and I called her over to come and help me look. The keys weren't anywhere! I was dreading having to call Bob and Kathy to tell them I'd lost the cash register keys, because once a set of register keys is lost, new ones have to be ordered from the manufacturer. I knew I hadn't put them anywhere different, but they weren't where they were supposed to me.

"By that time, I was angry with myself and had decided to just give up

the search and leave. I was on my way past the main store register —
and there were the keys. They were in that main register that I had
"Z"-ed out first, and the register had been turned on again. I had not
gone back to that register after "Z"-ing it, but the keys had somehow
left the vicinity of the second register, gone back into the main register, turned themselves in the lock, and turned the register on! It had
all happened right in front of me, and I hadn't seen a thing. I don't
know whether the keys floated across the room, or disappeared and
then reappeared in another part of the store, but I do know that they
got back into that main register without any help from me! I told my
sister, 'Stace — I've got my keys, now let's get out of here!'

"And then, one night, I actually saw a ghost. This was the same time
that the Schleimers had a Ouija board.

"I shared my upstairs apartment at the New Shoreham House with a
roommate, and we slept in bunk beds. One night, about 11:00, I came
upstairs and got into bed. My roommate, Cheryl, was asleep in the
upper bunk. After I was in bed, I began to hear voices, lots of them. It
sounded like a crowd. I couldn't make out what they were saying; the
voices were indistinct. The room faced the water, and at first I thought
the voices were from a party down on the waterfront.

"Then — as if through a tunnel — I heard a dog barking, a very distant sound. I actually couldn't tell if it was external or inside my head,
and I couldn't get up to look out, because I was scared. I decided I
must be having a dream, and I tried to tell myself, in the dream, to
look out the window.

"We had all our clothes hanging on a dowel rod in the room, and suddenly, all the clothes on that dowel started swaying back and forth.
The window was open, but there was no wind; the curtains didn't
move at all. I felt a chill all the way up and down my spine, and I felt
my heart beat fast, then slow down, and then I heard a loud clap —
like a handclap — as if someone was in the room. I looked: and there
was a new silhouette in the room, in addition to the furniture and
other familiar objects that I knew belonged there.

"It was the figure of a woman, with a full, bustled type of skirt, wearing a kerchief on her head. I opened and closed my eyes three times,
and the woman was still there. So, I moved to turn on the lamp next
to the bed. My neck and spine were completely stiff, and I almost
couldn't move, but I used all my strength and all my will power, and
managed to turn on the lamp.

"The woman was gone — but the clothes on the dowel were still moving back and forth, and there was no wind, no movement of the curtains at the windows.

"I felt a presence in that room. Even though my roommate was sound
asleep, I left the light on, and even with the light on, I still felt a

strange presence in the room. So I said, 'Why don't you just go now?'

"After that, I was able to sleep.

"The next day, I told Cheryl about the experience, and she told the Schleimers. And it was then that Kathy Schleimer started telling me about some of her experiences with things coming off the walls, and bathroom drawers and cupboards opening all by themselves.

"I never saw that woman with the bustled skirt in my room again, but I remember something that happened when Bob and Kathy started working with two Ouija boards at the New Shoreham House. Bob's mother and I worked one of the boards one night, and the pointer started jumping! We asked, 'Are there any spirits here?'

"The pointer spelled out, 'Yes.'

"'What are their names?' we asked.

"The answer came back, 'Elijah.'

"'What are you doing, Elijah?' we asked.

"'Searching,' was the answer.

"'Searching for what, Elijah?'

"'Peace.'

"After that, there was nothing more."

THE THING THAT GOES BUMP IN THE NIGHT
AND BRINGS BRACELETS

I FIRST CAUGHT SIGHT OF MY GHOST about 15 years ago," Lorraine Cyr told me in 1991. Lorraine grew up on the Island. She and her sister, Barbara, were nine and 11 years old when their parents, Ulric and Beatrice Cyr, bought the then-dilapidated Surf Hotel. Lorraine and Barbara worked with their parents, every afternoon after school, to help renovate the huge old seaside hotel, which opened for business on July 4, 1956. It has been a haven ever since for families who return, year after year.

Barbara and her husband, Stanley Nyzio, own the Gables Inn and Gables II. Lorraine runs the Surf Hotel with her parents, taking reservations all winter and presiding at the front desk all summer. She is generally accompanied by several of the cuddly, huge-eyed Cavalier King Charles spaniels that she breeds and shows.

Lorraine lives in a fairly new house that was built for her on the Ocean Avenue property bought by her parents in the early 1950s. In front of Lorraine's is a smaller house formerly known as Fair Winds, which was Ulric and Beatrice Cyr's first Block Island home. Ever resourceful, and with the help of Ulric's Coast Guard buddies, the Cyrs pre-fabricated the cottage on the lawn, then erected the finished sections. Recycled lights and windows were used, for a total building cost of $600.

The story that Lorraine told me in 1991, however, did not concern the Surf Hotel or Fair Winds, but her own relatively new house. We sat in her modern kitchen, a collection of vintage cribbage boards hanging on one wall, as Lorraine told me about her ghost.

"My niece, Stephanie Nyzio, was staying at my house with me," Lorraine began, describing her first ghost sighting in the mid-1970s. "One evening, we heard the siren going off for a fire alarm, so we drove out to see what was going on. As we were returning to the house, driving up the driveway, we saw something — Stephanie saw it first, then I did. It was a distinct profile of a man with a hat, walking across the front of the house. We could see him against the window. But then he disappeared. When we looked again, no one was there.

"Another time, my other niece, Karen Nyzio, was staying with me for the winter. She would find lamps on in her room, when she knew she'd left them all off. And one day, she came to me and asked, 'Did you leave this bracelet on my dresser?'

"She showed me a silver bracelet, an old one, that she had found on top of the dresser in her room. It hadn't been there before; it wasn't hers, and she had never seen it before then. And it was nothing of mine, and I'd never seen it. But there it was. We were the only two people in the house, and neither of us could explain where it came from or how it got there. To this day, Karen will not sleep in this house again.

"Then one summer, my cousin Beatrice stayed here with me. She was chambermaiding at the Surf, and her husband was night watchman there. He would always come home late, or rather very early in the morning, and she'd get on his case sometimes about waking her up when he came in, because she had to get up early for her job.

"One night, he came home late as usual. As he came into the room, all the window shades started flapping, the way they do in a wind, making a lot of noise. It woke Beatrice up. She was annoyed, because she hadn't opened the windows that far, and she thought he'd done it, and caused the noise. She complained, and told him she'd been asleep. He didn't say anything, but she felt him get into bed next to her. She couldn't sleep, so she got up and went into the bathroom. When she returned to the bedroom, the bed was empty. There was no one there. And, when she looked at the clock, she saw it was only 2:00 a.m., much too early for her husband to be coming home — he was still at his job. But she knew that someone had come into that room and gotten into that bed.

"Another time, in one of the bedroom closets upstairs, we found a pair of men's trousers, with little tiny black and white checks on them. They didn't belong to anyone who'd been staying here, and the style and pattern of the fabric weren't the kind of thing that people generally wear these days, anyway. They didn't fit anyone who had been here. None of us had any idea where they came from, or how they got there. We got rid of them.

"Then last year, there was a man staying here who didn't believe in ghosts. We'd told him some of the stories, but he just dismissed them as a lot of rubbish. One afternoon, he went upstairs to take a shower, and when he came down, he was really scared. The clock in his bedroom upstairs had suddenly started running backwards, fast, and wouldn't stop. No one saw it except him, but it really shook him up. I think maybe he believed in ghosts after that.

"Over the years, it's just been a lot of little things, like that. My friend Gladys, who was staying here for a week in February, heard something tapping on the wall two nights in a row. She said it sounded like Morse code, and she wished she'd had a book so she could decipher it. It wasn't coming from the window, she said. It was on an inside wall.

"And then my niece Stephanie was staying with me here one night. Her room was one of the upstairs corner rooms; I'll show you when we go up. One night, she heard something banging on the outside of the bedroom window. It sounded like a tree branch, and it woke her up, it was so loud. She got up and looked out, and saw the tree outside the window, saw the big branch that had been making so much noise.

Eventually, she got used to it and went back to sleep. When she woke up the next morning, though, she saw that there was no tree there at all, anywhere near that corner of the house. There never has been a tree there, as long as I've lived here. But she distinctly saw a big tree, with branches, right outside that window.

"There was another incident, too, with my gift closet upstairs. I have a closet where I keep all my wrapping paper, and when I have gifts to wrap, I do it in there. When I'm not using the closet, it's locked. One time, my parents were staying here with me. My mother and I had been wrapping a lot of gifts, and when we were finished, I locked the door to the closet and put the key away where I usually keep it. My parents don't know where I keep the key, and my mother didn't see me put it away.

"A day later, my mother went back up to the gift closet and found the door open, and the key in the lock. Now, none of us had gone into that closet. I'm the only one who knew where the key was, and I hadn't been in there since I'd locked it up the day before. But there it was, open, with the key in the door.

"Another thing I've noticed is that the board covering the opening to my attic is askew a lot, instead of fitted right over the opening, the way it should be. It gets lifted up, somehow, and turned, so it doesn't go back into place. That opening to the attic is inside a closet, and I keep the door to the closet closed. If it were a wind moving the board, it would have to be a very strong wind, coming up from underneath, to lift the board. But there's no way a wind could come through that closet, with the door shut all the time. And it's not vibrations, because the board sits down in a framework, and is heavy enough that a little vibration wouldn't bother it. And, vibration wouldn't lift it anyway, it would make it settle. I noticed just yesterday that the board was askew again, lifted up over the opening, and I haven't gotten up on the ladder yet to fix it."

"Are you sure you don't have a vagrant living here?" I asked Lorraine at this point.

"You know, I wondered that myself," she replied. "I'd heard a story about a house someplace where a man lived in the attic for years, and nobody knew it. So, I went up with a flashlight and looked through all my closets, and all around the attic. No one there, and no traces of anyone ever being there."

We went upstairs. "I always keep the door at the top of the stairs closed," Lorraine pointed out, "so my dogs and cats never come up here. I sleep downstairs, and I hear noises at night sometimes, like something dragging across the floor upstairs in the middle of the night. But I know it isn't the animals; they're all downstairs with me, and this door is shut.

"I have a lot of old furniture up here," Lorraine noted, of her handsome Victorian antiques. She shrugged. "Maybe whatever it is came with the furniture."

We entered the front, southeast corner bedroom. "This room is where the clock ran backwards," she said, "and the closet of this room is where we found the checked trousers that didn't belong to anybody." In the room just across the hall, to the rear of the house, was the closet with the opening to the attic. Lorraine opened the closet door and showed me the board across the attic opening. It was, indeed, turned and placed loosely on top of the opening, in a way no wind could do — if, indeed, a wind could get through that closed closet. "This room is where the bracelet was left on the dresser," she told me, "and this is the room where my cousin Beatrice felt the man get into bed next to her."

We continued to the front center bedroom. "This is the room where the lamps go on by themselves," Lorraine said.

The rear, northernmost bedroom is where Stephanie saw the huge tree outside the window. There is no tree there, nor any space for one, as the window where Stephanie saw the tree looks out over the garage roof.

I asked Lorraine if she ever felt frightened, living with something that goes bump in the night and brings bracelets.

"Never," she responded. "It stays upstairs and I stay downstairs. And I hardly even notice the dragging sounds at night any more, I've gotten so used to them."

POLTERGEIST AT MARTIN HOUSE?

HELEN HUBBARD HAS LIVED ON BLOCK ISLAND since 1982. A native of Middletown, Connecticut, she came to Block Island and, in her own words, stayed "Because I love it here!" When Helen was 17, majoring in child psychology at Mark Hopkins College in Brattleboro, Vermont, her friends nicknamed her "Hobbit." At the time, she explained to me, the college had accreditation issues and needed 5000 more books in the library. A list of books was circulated so that students might buy books to help stock the library. Helen had just read "everything that Tolkien ever wrote," she told me, and the other students teased her about reading "kids' stories." She rebutted, explaining that epic tales of good and evil written by an Oxford scholar weren't just for children. In reply, the other students just chanted, "Oh, hobbit, hobbit, hobbit!"

And so, Helen has been "Hobbit" ever since, in homage to the joyful, brave and industrious hobbits of Tolkien's books. Hobbit's careers on the Island have included working for the town road department, waitressing, bartending, and owning a housecleaning company called White Gloves. She has sung tenor in the Block Island Ecumenical Choir for nine years, traveling to Vienna with the choir in 1997.

"I had a ghost at Martin House," she told me quietly one evening last October, as we sat together in the Harbor Church waiting to be called for the first seating of the church's Roll Call dinner. A magnificent feast of turkey with all the trimmings, it is arguably the best church dinner anywhere.

Hobbit's reference to Martin House went back to her residency, for several years during the mid 1990s, on Ocean Avenue. She lived in one of the front apartments at Martin House, the compact quadriplex built by Block Island Economic Development, or BIED.

Perhaps it is not coincidental that Martin House is next door to Lorraine Cyr's property, where some odd events have taken place.

Hobbit continued, "At the time, I bartended on Tuesday nights at the Beachead. One Tuesday, I was taking a nap before a night shift when I heard a group of people standing next to my bed, speaking to each other. I wondered at first if they could be outside. It was a warm night, and the windows were open. The conversation had been soft and indistinct, but just then I heard someone say, 'Don't worry, she's asleep.'

"And then — I felt someone sit on the bed. I could feel the side of the mattress next to me going down with the added weight of somebody else on that bed.

"A moment later, I felt two hands on my back, rolling me onto my stomach! I opened my eyes and turned my head to look, and there was no one there. The hair on my arms was standing straight up, and in a few seconds, so was I! I put one foot on the floor, took one step and I was out the door and into my car. I went straight to the house of my friend, Janet Ziegler, on High Street.

"When I told her what had happened, she said, 'Oh, you must have been dreaming! There's no such thing as ghosts!'

"I said, 'Then why is my hair standing straight up? I think I might just have a poltergeist at my place, and they're not always friendly! And anyway, I didn't feel like sticking around to find out!"

Hobbit continued, as we sat in the church waiting for the Roll Call dinner to start, "There was another occasion, too.

"I had a cat given to me while I was at Martin House, a 'boy cat' that had kittens 10 weeks later. One afternoon I was in the kitchen, and there was a cardboard box upside down on the floor. All of a sudden, the box started to scoot around on the linoleum. I thought the kittens were playing inside it.

"I picked up the box, and there was nothing inside! And the kittens were asleep in the living room, on the couch, next to their mommy.

"I decided then that I definitely had a poltergeist in that house! I took the box outside and got rid of it, so my poltergeist would have one less toy to play with.

"My first thought was that some spirits had come over from Lorraine Cyr's house. I told my story to Gail Nivers, who works for Barbara and Stanley Nyzio at The Gables Inn. She's stayed at Lorraine's house quite a lot, and she told me, 'Oh, yes, there's all sorts of ghostly stuff going on at Lorraine's!'

"I didn't have any other ghostly visits while I lived at Martin House, but those two were quite enough for me. I haven't experienced any poltergeists — or whatever they were — since I moved out of that apartment, and I'm quite happy without them!"

A HAPPY SPIRIT AT THE SURF HOTEL?

I WAS AT THE SURF HOTEL ONE AFTERNOON in the early fall, about 1998, talking with Ulric and Beatrice Cyr, the hotel's owners. I was doing an article on the Surf, and in the 13 years I'd lived on the Island and known the Cyr family, I had never seen the upstairs of the hotel. A hotel employee, Mickey Terrana, was there that day, helping to show me around.

"We have a ghost here," he volunteered, as we all sat in the Surf's breakfast room, behind the front desk area.

"You do?" I smiled at Bea Cyr. "You never told me that."

"Well," Bea gave a gentle shrug of her slender shoulders. She is an elegant, understated woman who wears her crown of white hair on top of her head and regards the world quietly from deep-set eyes. There is no nonsense about her. "Sometimes, sitting in the kitchen, I've felt a shadow behind me and had the feeling somebody was there."

"I've had that feeling, too," said Ulric, a genial, blue-eyed man with a huge, friendly smile. "But I never gave it much thought."

"I've seen it," said Mickey earnestly. "At least, when I've been down in the cellar, I've seen someone, or something, running through there."

I was on a fact-finding mission that day, not a ghostly one. But six years later, I called Lorraine Cyr to ask her about the Surf Hotel ghost.

"I've never seen or experienced anything," she told me. "But we've had employees and guests who have said they've seen things. Nothing big, nothing extravagant. People have reported seeing a woman in a long white dress. Aren't they always in a long dress?" she laughed. "And people have said they've seen someone or something in the third floor hallway."

She continued, "Our night watchmen have had people ask them, 'Did you see those people come in, in Victorian dress?'

"And once, a guest heard a radio playing, but there was no radio around, and nobody else there, either.

"Just little things, nothing big, nothing definite, certainly nothing scary," she summed up. "And nothing that I've ever seen."

"When I first came here in 1997 and interviewed at the Surf," Mickey Terrana told me in November 2004, "I thought to myself, 'This place has to have a ghost in it.' I could feel it.

"Wayne Battey and his wife were living here then, at Surfside. Wayne used to talk to himself. He said he was talking to 'the ghost — Aunt Jennie.'"

Mickey continued, "Time went by. The Cyrs got to know me, and I got to know them. I was doing night watch at the hotel one or two nights a week, and also working days.

"One night, about two or three a.m., I was watching TV at the hotel desk. I turned my head, and out of the corner of my eye, I saw a tall woman with a white dress, high white collar, dark hair in a bun on top of her head and a hat. She walked through the lobby, from the back door to the front.

"The next day, I described her to the Cyrs. 'Oh, that sounds like Aunt Jennie,' they said. 'She used to work here.'

"On my breaks during the day, I used to sit on the staircase, three or four stairs up, and talk to Lorraine while she sat at the front desk. She told me, 'That's where Aunt Jennie used to sit.'

"In the kitchen, in the mornings,' Mickey added, "the family and staff used to sit around the table for breakfast, and Stanley cooked." Stanley, Beatrice and Ulric's son-in-law, is married to Barbara, Lorraine's sister. The Nyzios own the Gables Inn and Gables II, and Stanley is one of the very few people, besides herself, that Beatrice will allow to cook in her kitchen.

"One morning, Mrs. Cyr said to me, 'You know, Mickey, I think you're right about the ghost — I was in the kitchen, and I could see something white walking past, down the stairway and through the wall.'"

"Other people have seen a mysterious lady in gray on the porch from time to time, and mentioned her to us," Mickey concluded. "I suppose it's Aunt Jennie again."

If there is any ghost at the Surf, it would have to be a gentle, contented spirit, given the happy atmosphere fostered there by the Cyrs, who have owned the hotel almost 50 years.

In 1955, when Ulric Cyr was four years away from his retirement after a 20-year career in the U.S. Coast Guard, he was thinking about what he would do next. Ulric had grown up in a family tradition of Block Island hospitality. His father, Elphege Cyr, built the Sea Breeze Inn on Spring Street with lumber from the old Adrian Hotel annex, and each day after school Ulric and his sisters were set to work removing the old square nails from the lumber. Ulric's family owned and operated Cyr's Sea Breeze for 40 years.

Strolling on Crescent Beach one Sunday in 1955 with his wife, Beatrice, and his sister, Madeleine, Ulric looked up at the Surf and saw an opportunity. "The Surf," he now maintains, "was our best choice, once we had seen the views from inside and considered the possibilities."

To others, the building might have seemed a hopeless derelict. Damaged in the 1938 hurricane and closed for 17 years, the 80-year-old structure was sagging and full of holes, with a porch that was ready to fall into the ocean. "My mother sat down and cried when she first saw it," Bea Cyr once told me. "We had just built a house, and she said, 'You sold your beautiful house to buy *this*?'"

"This" was actually an amalgam of 19th-century buildings, the oldest section on the east end having been built as a residence for New Shoreham's resident physician, Dr. Mann, in 1873. Put on the market three years later, "Surf Cottage," as it was then known, was opened as a new hotel in 1879 by Postmaster C.W. Willis. Business boomed during that heyday of steamboat travel to the Island, and five years later a center addition was built, surrounded by eight-foot-wide verandas and topped by a cupola. In 1888, Mr. Willis built a four-story addition on the west end, "rendering Surf Cottage one of the largest hotels on the Island," according to the contemporary account in the *Providence Journal*. The hotel's quirky, rambling, quite delightful architecture remains the same today as it was in 1888.

After lots of carpentry, patching, plumbing, masonry, refinishing, wiring, wallpapering and other renovation — all done by family members, including the Cyrs' daughters, 9-year old Lorraine and 11-year-old Barbara — the Cyrs opened the first floor of their new hotel on July 4, 1956. The dining room served three meals a day back then and was open to the public. Beatrice did all the cooking, and was famous for it — guests still recall that the hardest part of ending their vacations was going back to their own home cooking. Though the hotel now serves only breakfast and is not open for public meals, Beatrice still rules her kitchen, and allows only family members to cook there.

To many of Block Island's perennial summer visitors, the Surf became home, and has remained so for years. Loyal guests reserve the same weeks and the same rooms from one summer to the next. Families hold vacation reunions — often barbecue get-togethers at the grills out back — with other families who have grown up alongside them. On a typical evening, the Cyrs will play board games with guests in the hotel's old-fashioned parlor. The Surf is, simply, a family kind of place, the place where the Cyrs' own daughters grew up, and a way of life for its guests.

So, if there is indeed a resident spirit at the Surf, it must surely be a "high spirit," happily existing on the aromas of Bea's cooking, watching children at play, and perhaps kibitzing at a board game or two.

THE PERFUMED LADY OF CALICO HILL

I T STARTED IN MAY 1971," Scott Fowler began, as he recounted the experiences of his family at their house on Calico Hill. Scott has spent much of his life on Block Island. He works for the Block Island Power Company, and he and his wife, Sheila, have raised their own family here. A reserved, rather shy man who is quietly helpful to others while shunning the limelight for himself, Scott is not given to story-telling.

He continued, "My parents had moved here while I was in the army, to a house on Calico Hill called the Cora Hall House. Two sisters had once lived in the house, I'm not sure exactly when, and there was a story that one of them, Cora, had drowned herself in the surf. I don't know if that has anything to do with my story or not. Anyway, the house was in terrible shape when my parents bought it, and they completely renovated it inside.

"I came to the Island and stayed with my parents for two months after they'd renovated. My room was the southwest bedroom, just to the left at the top of the stairs. One night, I was asleep in my room and something woke me up. The room was cold, and damp, and it felt as if someone or something was sitting on top of the bed. I tried to pull the covers up, but I couldn't move them.

"And then I saw, sitting at the end of the bed, a form. It was a woman. Her hair was done up in a bun, and her clothes were those of a hundred years ago, or more: a high-collar top, with puffy long sleeves. There was also a vague notion of perfume in the air. I couldn't move or make a noise. I don't know how long this lasted — long enough, that's for sure — but then the woman disappeared.

"I didn't tell anyone about this experience, and nothing more happened until two weeks later, at about 4:30 in the morning Again, I woke up, and the same woman was standing in the doorway of the room. I found that I was able to scream— and I did. She went away, but there was a heavy perfume smell all through the upstairs.

"I did say something about it this time; the next morning, I asked my sister, who slept in the next room, if she had ever seen or experienced anything strange in that house. Her immediate reaction was, 'Mom — he saw her, he saw her!' My sister had seen the same woman, with old-fashioned clothes and her hair in a bun, and had smelled the same perfume smell.

"We saw the lady about four more times, over the next seven years, and then, after 1978, she didn't seem to visit any more. Nothing bad ever happened; we just saw her, and experienced her presence — and the smell of her perfume."

WHO ROAMS HIGH IN ATALANTA, AT THE HIGHVIEW?

G ARY HAS GHOST STORIES ABOUT THE HIGHVIEW!" Rally reported to me on a February afternoon in 2005, after he'd been to the Block Island Grocery. Rally easily makes an hour-long excursion out of a trip to the grocery or post office. A master of the downtown Island social encounter, his stock in trade is all sorts of information, which he delights in exchanging every place he goes. He stops and chats with everyone at the store's deli counter, including manager Gary Ryan, who always wears a smile. Part of Gary's hospitality ethic stems from the late 1980s and early 1990s, when he was a partner and chef at the Highview Inn.

I was on the phone to Gary the next day, and met with him and his wife, Bonny, at their Pilot Hill home on a wet and stormy Valentine's Day afternoon.

The Ryans came to Block Island in 1986 with their four young children, Eric, Jordan, Sean and Hillary. The young family had lived on Long Island; Gary, an optician, commuted four hours every day to his New York City office. A turning point for the Ryans occurred when Gary was diagnosed with thyroid and parathyroid cancer in the mid-1980s. Medical treatment was timely and proved successful, but the Ryans were ready for a lifestyle change.

Meanwhile, Bonny Ryan's mother, Lillian Seamon, had been contacted by her niece, Marilyn ("Wolfie") Wolfe, about a business opportunity on Block Island. The Highview Inn was for sale, and Wolfie wanted Lillian and her husband, Jerome, to buy into the business in partnership with her. The Seamons already had a house in Ministers Lot, bought in the 1960s at their niece's urging.

"Oh, I don't know — only if Bonny and Gary go, too," Lillian told Wolfie.

"We jumped at the opportunity!" Bonny recounted the story to me. "We bought the Highview in September of 1985, with my parents and Wolfie. Gary was operated on in November. We sold our Long Island house on Christmas Eve, and we moved to Block Island in February 1986. Gary spent March and April that year refinishing the dining room at the Highview. It's still one of the prettiest dining rooms on the Island."

Bonnie's parents moved to Block Island in March. Sadly, Jerome Seamon died one week after the move.

The four remaining business partners owned the Highview for more than a decade. "We all shared responsibilities," said Gary, though he was the designated chef while the others pitched in at the desk and telephone, room-cleaning, bartending and various other duties. The

Inn was old-fashioned in style, with shared baths. The restaurant had enjoyed a good reputation for many years, and the new partners maintained it.

"I remember two stories about the Highview, from the late 1980s," Gary told me. "Two different people had strange experiences. Both were young women in their twenties, and both stayed in the same room. These incidents were several years apart, and the two women didn't know each other.

"The guest rooms had all been given the names of ships, and the room where odd events seemed always to occur was called Atalanta. It was a corner room, up on the third floor."

"It was a bizarre room," agreed Bonny. "No matter what kind of people stayed in it, strange things were reported about that room."

"One event," continued Gary, "occurred when one of the two young women that I mentioned was upstairs in Atalanta, lying in bed. She looked up, and saw an apparition of a young girl in a white dress going past the open door of the room. She said it was a form, not a solid person. It was definitely the form of a young girl, definitely in white, and it seemed to be floating past the door. The woman got really hysterical after she saw it, and she ran downstairs.

"The second incident that I heard about happened in that same room. As I said, it was a different woman staying there, and a different year. This time, the woman was lying in bed, reading a newspaper. While she was reading it, the paper suddenly ripped in half — all by itself."

"When Sarah Finke was the speech pathologist at the school, she stayed at the Highview each time she made one of her trips to the Island," said Bonny. "At least, she did when we owned it.

"Sarah stayed in a room on the first floor. She said that she had the experience, when walking up the stairs to her room, of feeling a presence next to her: 'Someone was walking up there with me,' she told me. She said it was definitely female, and when she said something to it, the presence disappeared."

"We had to give her credit for staying in that building all by herself in the middle of winter," added Gary.

Bonny had her own experience in the old hotel. "I remember one day when I was up in Atalanta, making beds," she said. "I felt a draft blowing through, like air coming from outside, through an open window. Except the window wasn't open. There was no breeze coming in, and no reason for any draft."

When Gary told me the stories of the two young women having experiences years apart in Atalanta, he said, "It sticks in my mind that one of them might have been Liz Cowles's sister, Stacey, but I'm really not sure. Her name comes to mind, for some reason."

Liz Cowles, owner of the boutique Distant Shores, under the National

Hotel, had worked at Esta's gift shop for a number of years before starting her own business. Liz, years ago, had told me several stories about Esta's and the New Shoreham House.

I called Liz, and asked her about the Highview. "Stacey and I rented a room on the top floor of the Highview during the late 1980s, when we both worked at Esta's," she told me. "The room had two beds, a sink in the corner with a mirror above it, and a bathroom in the hall that was shared with other rooms.

"Stacey and I would consistently hear an odd noise; it sounded like a wooden pencil, or a quarter, rolling across the floor. We would hear it at least three times a week, at different times: sometimes after dinner, when we were sitting in the room reading, sometimes in the middle of the night if we got up to go to the bathroom. It was strange, unpredictable. We never saw or found anything that would make that noise, and we always remarked on it to each other. It was like something trapped in the floor." She added that Stacey had experienced a couple of odd events in the room.

"Oh, yes, I remember that room at the Highview!" responded Stacey Marsh, when I reached her at her home in Albany, New York. Stacey, too, cited the odd noise, like that of a pencil or a quarter rolling across the floor: "Sometimes it would wake us up, and we'd say, 'Oh, yeah, there's that noise again!'"

She added, "I experienced two distinct things in that room," and proceeded to tell me about them. Both were different from the occurrences previously described to me by Gary Ryan.

"One time," said Stacey," I was sitting in the room, writing a letter to a friend. It was a two-page letter, and I was holding a page in each hand, reading it over.

"As I held that letter, I felt hands on me, a hand on each of my forearms. It was as if someone was standing in front of me, pushing my arms apart. I very clearly felt those hands on me, pushing — there's no other way to explain it. And there was no one there. At that point, I decided, 'Yep, time to get out of here for awhile!'

"The other experience occurred at the sink. I was getting ready for bed one night when I was really tired, washing my face at the sink. I suddenly found myself staring into the mirror. I heard a voice talking, and after awhile I realized it was my voice — but I wasn't talking! I felt that someone was channeling through me. It was very strange, listening to that voice, realizing it was my own, but I wasn't saying anything. I had a sense of time passing — I have no idea how long I was there, looking into the mirror and hearing the voice, but it seemed that I had been there awhile. I couldn't tell what the voice was saying, even though I felt like an observer, and it was my voice. It was a very weird feeling.

"I'd always had a vague belief in ghosts, but those are two experiences that I remember, crystal clear. I was very scared sometimes in that room, but I never felt that there was anything really bad there."

Stacey added, "Oh, and there was one other thing. When Liz and I worked at Esta's, the store used to sell seashell wind chimes. We put some of those wind chimes in our room at the Highview. There would be times in our room when the curtain was perfectly still, but the chimes would be moving and ringing without any wind."

Relatively little has been written about the history of the Highview. Originally called the Connecticut House, a name it kept for ten years, the hotel was built in 1878. The first owner, Gary Ryan told me, was M.M. Day. Gary said that when he was refinishing the front desk area in the l980s, he found a place where M.M. Day had carved his name in the wood of the building, above the desk. "I suppose it's still there," he shrugged.

M.M. Day died a few years after the hotel was built, and it was taken over by his wife and son. The 1977 book, *Research, Reflection and Recollections of Block Island*, by Fred Benson, mentions Jennie Day as an early owner of the Connecticut House; she was probably M.M. Day's widow. The first hotel guest register, dating from 1878 to the 1890s, records the name of owner Elmer H. Day, probably the son.

Also recorded in the register are some names of distinction: President Benjamin Harrison signed in on December 1, 1890, and President Grover Cleveland on August 3, 1893.

Gary told me that the White House Marching Band, and boxer John L. Sullivan, had also stayed at the hotel during those years.

"The Highview," he remarked, "is the second oldest continuously-operating hotel on the Island. The oldest is the Spring House." He added that the Highview has had relatively few owners since the Days owned it; it had passed through the hands of only four other owners when it was sold to the Ryans and Seamons.

No discussion of the Highview is complete without some mention of the impressive Wetherbee murals and paintings that adorn the walls of the hotel. Itinerant artist H. D. Wetherbee came to the Island in the late 1940s with Captain Gene Stinson and his son, Stanley. The Stinsons were swordfishermen, and they took Wetherbee, then about 50 years old, fishing aboard their boat, the *Stanley*.

The Stinsons lived across the road and down the hill from the Highview, and Wetherbee settled in at the hotel, which was then undergoing renovation. In exchange for room and board and a bottle of Scotch each day, Wetherbee painted wonderful images of Island life on the walls of the hotel's guest rooms, dining room and ground floor bar. The artist's daily routine was to sketch at various locations on the Island in the morning — sketching on paper bags or whatever came to hand — paint at the Highview in the afternoon, and enjoy his bottle of

Scotch in the evening. His Highview paintings were created in 1948 and 1949.

Wetherbee seemed to recognize that life on Block Island was different, and that it couldn't last forever. His paintings capture the way of life and the familiar faces in the fishing port. The colors and spareness of the late-1940s Island landscape, from the West Side to the old Island center, New Harbor and Old Harbor, characterize his work. Wetherbee's portraits of actual swordfishermen of the day are unmistakable to those who knew them, the faces and figures endowed with the personalities of the people represented.

Wetherbee's paintings at the Highview include two dozen individual images in the bedrooms, featuring fishing boats and Island scenes. In the dining room are nine large-scale images, prominently featuring the swordfishing Stinsons, as befits a restaurant that built a reputation on Block Island swordfish. In the ground floor bar, now known as Club Soda, a mural depicting Island landscapes winds its way across all the walls, surrounding the beholder with a Block Island of the past. The paintings are priceless; many, particularly in the bar, have deteriorated over the years. Some have been reproduced as prints, and are available at Island galleries.

Wetherbee left the Island in the early 1950s. Gary said that he met Wetherbee's nephew during the time the Ryans had the Highview. The nephew told him that his uncle had died alone and homeless in the 1980s on the streets of New York.

Whatever pieces of the past may linger in the Highview, Gary Ryan maintains that he doesn't believe in ghosts. Still, he believes that there is "something" in the Highview, some presence, certainly in the room known as Atalanta. "The building definitely has its creaks, and things move," he said.

Some spirits on Spring Street

W E'RE GOING TO GO TELL GHOST STORIES TONIGHT!" announced Rally with a big grin, as the two of us seated ourselves at our favorite table at The Beachead. His remark was directed to Heather Sniffen, our waitress that evening. It was October 22, 2004, and Rally and I had been invited to tell ghost stories to a group of school students at the Island Free Library, as part of a "Night of Fright." The program was one of a series of participatory, game and storytelling evenings conducted for that age group by librarian Amy Dugan; the ghost stories were to be followed by pizza, then by some ghostly story writing or storytelling on the part of the students.

"Ooh," Heather responded, her black-fringed hazel eyes lighting up. "I have some ghosts!" She leaned slightly forward over our table, her long auburn/brown ringlets forming a frame around her face.

"When I was younger," she continued, "I had a summer job at the Spring House. A bunch of us kids, all about the same age, were working there that year. One thing that kept happening was that the light in the hall on the third floor of the hotel would go on by itself, and stay on. No matter how often we shut it off, it would always come on again by itself.

"One night, a group of us got together and decided, 'This is it — we are going to shut off that light, and we are going to do it together so we'll all *know* we shut it off!' So we all went to the switch for that particuler light, turned it off, and made sure it was off.

"But the light turned itself back on anyway, and stayed on. At that point, we all just decided, 'Okay, it wants to be on,' and we let it go. It was more determined than we were, and it had been there a lot longer."

"I used to see things at my parents' house, up on Spring Street, too," said Heather. Heather is the cousin of Karin Lord Carlone, who had some eerie experiences at the North Light; Heather's father, Jim, is the brother of Karin's mother, Barbara. The Sniffen house was purchased in the 1940s by Jim and Barbara's parents.

Continued Heather, "In my parents' house, I used to see two strange people: there was a woman, dressed in long, old-fashioned clothes, with her hair up in a bun, and there was a man in a top hat, with a mustache and a black coat. Once I woke in the middle of the night, and they were there in my room. The woman was sitting in the rocking chair, rocking, and the man was standing near her.

"I closed my eyes, and when I opened them again, the two people were gone. But the chair was still rocking.

"Then there's the story about the chair and the attic door," Heather added. "I'm not sure whether my parents or my grandparents told me

85

this. The attic has a trap door that you have to push open from the ceiling below to get inside the attic. Sometimes, when family members tried to open the trap door, the chair was directly on top of it. I guess they finally got the chair out of there so it wouldn't always be in the way."

"So, are you getting enough ghost stories?" Jim Sniffen asked me one day, as we met at the door of the Block Island Grocery. It was December 14, more than a month since my conversation with Heather at the Beachead. I'd left a couple of messages inquiring about house ghosts on the Sniffens' answering machine, but it was the holiday season, and everyone was busy with matters more immediate and pressing than the supernatural.

"What about your house? Any ghosts there?" I asked him with an encouraging smile.

"No, Beverly doesn't think so," he told me.

"Heather told me she's seen things there," I replied.

"Oh, yeah, she sees things — if Heather says we have ghosts, go right ahead and write about them!" he said, with a chuckle.

A few days later, returning to the Island from a brief trip to the mainland, I saw Beverly Sniffen aboard the *Block Island*. "So tell me, do you have ghosts in your house?" I asked her, sitting uninvited at her table. An artist and craftswoman who makes Block Island pendants of stained glass and Christmas tree ornaments from tiny starfish, Beverly was leafing through what appeared to be an arts and crafts book.

"I've never felt anything in the Block Island house," she replied, regarding me gravely. "But in our old house, in Monroe, Connecticut, there was a ghost. I used to feel her presence upstairs, in my sewing room. I knew she was there, and I would say hello to her.

"The day we left the house, I was vacuuming downstairs, and she came down to be with me. I think she knew we were saying good-bye.

"The closing on the house was awful!" Beverly continued. "It almost didn't happen. My lawyer told me that the buyer had wanted a clause guaranteeing the absence of ghosts in the house. It didn't go into the contract — but if she'd insisted, she wouldn't have gotten that house! I really didn't want her to have it — but now that she does, I'm almost certain she can't sense the ghost's presence. I don't think she would be able to.

"The Monroe ghost was always just a gentle presence, never anything scary," concluded Beverly. "I was very aware of her. If there were anything here in our house on Block Island, I think I would know it, or sense it."

At the end of that December, Rally and I once again found ourselves at the Beachead, being seated by Heather Sniffen. She told me with a laugh, "My sister Holly was here for Christmas, and my mother said to us, 'I don't know why Fran wants to write about this house. It's not haunted!'

"Holly just looked at her, and said, 'Yes it *is*, Mom!' Like, 'don't you *know* that?' I thought it was pretty funny."

The Coast Guard ghost

"How shall I start this Coast Guard story?" mused Building Official Marc Tillson, sitting in his office at Town Hall one Friday morning in April 2004. Marc is a cheerful, no-nonsense professional who deals in tangibles: boards, bricks, measurements, building specifications, zoning regulations. A self-described "neat-nick," he enjoys order, precision, and facts.

Marc has held his position with the Town for nearly two decades. He lives in and oversees the old Coast Guard Station, situated at the end of Champlin's Road, overlooking the entrance to the Great Salt Pond. Built in 1935, the Coast Guard Station is a three-building complex: the main house, the boathouse, and an equipment shed, added in 1938.

The three-story main house, with its prominent central light tower, is the best known and most conspicuous of the buildings on the property. During the summer, rooms in this building are rented to seasonal Town employees. In the winter, Marc is the sole occupant, living in the ground floor apartment that he built himself. His large tomcat, Big Fuzzy Thing, keeps him company.

"When I first moved into the Coast Guard Station, it was like any old building, with its share of creaks, bumps, noises, and 'things that go boo in the night,'" said Marc. "I ignored all of them, though I did notice a recurring noise at the base of the tower. It sounded like somebody going up and down the tower stairs. I noticed it, but when I heard that or any other sound at night, I just pulled the covers over my head and went back to sleep.

"During the summers, when other people lived in the house, they reacted to the house in odd ways. A couple of the women living there were scared to go upstairs; they didn't like to be around the corridor where the tower is.

"Another year, on one summer day, a woman was here with her mother, visiting the building. She walked upstairs, but came right down again; she said she was scared to stay upstairs, on the second floor.

"In addition to the footsteps on the tower stairs, another sound that could be heard was the sound of men's voices, carrying on conversations in a low rumble. One night, I woke up and heard that noise over my head. I was about to turn over and go back to sleep, but then I noticed that my cat, who is big and looks like a Maine coon cat, was sitting in the middle of the floor, staring up at the place where the noise was coming from. I thought that was pretty interesting — but I still went back to sleep.

"Very often, Coast Guard members who were once active at the Block Island station will stop by; we get these visitors every summer. A gentleman who visited the station one summer had been active there in the mid to late 1950s, and he was the one who told me the mad cook story.

"He told me that the men stationed there at the time began to notice that things were missing from the kitchen: knives, and silverware. They also noticed that the cook was becoming temperamental and difficult to get along with. He'd fly into rages, he'd sulk, he'd withdraw; he went into a whole pattern of irrational behavior.

"Eventually, he locked himself in a room on the second floor, with all the knives and silverware that had gone missing from the kitchen. They tried to get him to come out, but he wouldn't respond. Finally, a ladder was placed outside for access to the window of that second floor room. They went in, restrained the cook, put him into a strait-jacket, and took him away.

"It's interesting how stories get pieced together, a bit here and a bit there. In the summer of 2003, an elderly couple visited the Coast Guard property. The husband had been stationed here in the 1950s, at about the same time as the man who told me about the mad cook.

"The Coast Guard member who visited in 2003 had unfortunately had a stroke and couldn't talk that much, but his wife was very alert and communicative. I asked if they had heard the story of the mad cook.

"'Norman?!'" she immediately exclaimed. "Oh, of course!"

"And so, I've now named that spirit Norman, the mad cook," said Marc.

He continued, "I don't believe in ghosts, I never have. I've just always ignored the noises, and gone back to sleep, or back to whatever I was doing. The footsteps and the rumble of men's voices have been heard at all seasons, in all kinds of weather, when other people have been in the house, and when they haven't.

"Two years ago, I did have an odd experience, however. I'd been off shopping for the day, and I came home on the late boat with my bags of groceries and other things. I was the only one living in the house at the time.

"I unloaded the bags, brought them into the kitchen, and put them on the floor. As I was putting things away, I opened the silverware drawer. The drawer has a divider in it, with separate compartments for knives, forks, and spoons, to keep everything in order. When I opened the drawer, I saw that all the silverware had been messed up! Nothing was missing, but everything was out of place, as though it had just been thrown around in the drawer. I knew I hadn't left it that way, and no one else was living there. There was no rational way to explain it, and I thought that after the stories about Norman, the mad cook, it was an interesting occurrence.

"Another thing: about four years ago, there was a young couple living over at Beane Point, at the U.S. Fish & Wildlife property. The girl worked at night, at one of the restaurants. The easiest way for them to access the rest of the island was by water, because it's such a long way around by land, and so they used to kayak back and forth from the point. The closest property to theirs, by kayak, was of course the Coast Guard Station.

"One day, the girl said to me, 'Do you know that at night, there is sometimes a green glow coming from the tower of the station?'

"I said I hadn't seen or heard of any green light — yet.

"She said, 'Oh yes, we've seen it several times, from over at the point! It starts at the base of the tower and goes up; it's very eerie!' She told me that she was always skittish being on the Coast Guard property at night.

"It's been interesting," Marc concluded, "all the different stories that have come up over the years, the various experiences that people have had at the station, the fears of the seecond floor, and of course Norman, the mad cook. I think every old Coast Guard station should have a ghost! It's part of the atmosphere.

"I still hear the footsteps, and the low, muffled men's voices from time to time, on any kind of night, often when I know I'm the only person in the building. As you know, the Coast Guard building has an alarm system that detects any kind of intrusion or motion, but the noises are still there. It keeps life interesting."

The supervisory spirit of Corn Neck

DICK LEMOI IS A RETIRED RHODE ISLAND state trooper who once served as the Island's police chief, and he is not afraid of much of anything. He and his wife, Sheila, lived on the Island for many years, at their house on Center Road. Sheila was the owner and originator of Sheila's of Block Island, the boutique that formerly occupied the tiny house between the Surf Hotel and the Blue Dory. Sheila's parents, the McAloons, once owned an undertaking business on Old Town Road, and her brother, Vincent McAloon, built the former Neptune House into timeshare units.

Dick Lemoi loved to be on the water, and for a few summers ran fishing charter excursions on his boat. Eventually, the Lemois sold their Block Island house and chose life on a comfortable trawler, traveling between Block Island and Florida or the Bahamas every year. During their summers on the Island, Dick and Sheila kept their boat at the Block Island Boat Basin and managed the marina dock for Rally. Since those years, the Lemois have opted for the landlubbers' life again, and have built a new house on the east coast of Florida.

It was during the time that Dick worked as dockmaster at the Block Island Boat Basin that he told me this story.

"Some years back," recalled Dick, "I did some work on boilers in people's houses. One day, Sherm Dodge came to me and asked if I'd look at the boiler in one of the houses he took care of, on the east side of Corn Neck Road, just across from the entrance to West Beach Road. So I told him I'd go up and take a look at it."

Sherm Dodge, a direct descendant one of Block Island's 16 founders, Trustrum Dodge, is the late father of Willis Dodge. Willis and his wife, Edrie, run a B&B called Sunset Hill.

"Well, I went up to the house on the Neck," continued Dick, "and into the basement. I started working on the boiler. And after a little while, I got the feeling that someone was there with me, watching me. I felt that I wasn't alone. I looked around, and nobody was there — so I went back to work on the boiler, and again, I got that same feeling, as if I was being watched by someone else who was in the room with me. I looked all around again, and there was still nobody there. So, I finished the job, but all the time I had that feeling of someone else being there.

"I mentioned it to Sherm later, and he said, 'Oh, yes, didn't you know? Somebody died in that house once — hanged himself in the basement. That's who it was!'

"I've never been back in that house since," concluded Dick, "and I've never wanted to go back.

"I *know* there was someone there with me!"

This North Light "Keeper" Has Dog Issues

T WO OF THE PASSENGERS BOUND for the mainland aboard the *Block Island* on October 29, 2004 were New Shoreham Chief of Police Vincent Carlone and his Irish wolfhound, Wallace. Two other passengers were my husband, Rally, and myself.

A habitual wanderer when aboard the boat, Rally roamed the cabin, sat with the chief for awhile, and quickly made friends with the imposingly tall but very affable Wallace. Midway into the trip, Rally leaned over the seat where I was reading and reported excitedly, "Vin says that his wife has a ghost story about the North Light, and he says it's a good one!" Hastily, I scribbled a note to call the chief when we were all back on the Island.

I caught up with Chief Carlone at the police station a week later via phone, in the midst of one of his busy days. When told that the call had nothing to do with business, Carlone laughed and replied, "Oh good, that's the best kind!"

I explained that I would like to follow up on the North Light ghost story with his wife, Karin. She, as it turned out, spends most of the week off-Island, teaching sixth grade at St. Philomena's School in Portsmouth, Rhode Island.

The chief responded enthusiastically. "An important thing about Karin: she is absolutely incapable of telling a lie. It is the way she is, the way she was brought up, the way her family is. I've tested her many times. Every single time she tells this story, it is exactly the same, down to the last detail. It is very convincing."

Later that month, on Sunday of Thanksgiving weekend, Karin was able to meet with me. It was a cold, gray, rainy afternoon when I arrived at the house on Cormorant Cove that the Carlones had rented for the winter. Inside, the warmth of daily life prevailed. Karin, a slender woman with long-flowing, light brown hair and a quietly serious demeanor, had been busy at her computer with a teaching project. Wallace was as friendly as ever.

"It's funny, my friend Tamzen just called a little while ago to tell me she's all alone at the North Light," said Karin, as we sat at the dining room table. "The lighthouse is being closed for the season, and she's up there waiting for the plumber, Bill Vallee. I asked her if she was afraid, but she said no, not really. We've been friends for years, but I never told her that story before last weekend." Tamzen is Tamzen Mazzur, whose family roots go back a very long way on Block Island. Tamzen lives with her mother, Marceline Mazzur, on High Street, and manages the Block Island Health and General Store in the winter.

As it turned out, Karin Lord Carlone's own family goes back at least two generations on Block Island. Her grandparents, she told me, used to visit the Island in the summers and live on their boat, but her grandmother wanted a house. "This was in the 1940s. They bought an old house up on Spring Street, near the Spring House. It belongs to the Sniffens now; Jim Sniffen is my uncle, my mother's brother." The Carlones had had Thanksgiving dinner with the Sniffens three days before our interview. "We always used to get together for holidays," Karin told me. "There were six children in their family and two in ours, my sister Heidi and myself. We used to call them 'cousins by the dozens.'"

Karin eased into her story of the North Light: "When my sister and I were a lot younger, six or seven years old, our family used to like to walk out to the North Light every summer. The North Light was boarded up in those days, but there were ways to get in, and everyone used to go inside. When we went there, we liked to climb all the way up to the tower.

"The building had been abandoned, and it was a place that looked haunted. Inside, there were ripped curtains at the windows, and closets with things still hanging in them. There were holes in the plaster walls, and you could see through them to the horsehair and wood beneath. My father would always joke about a ghost living in the lighthouse, and he even had a name for him: 'Foul Fellow Finnegan O'Toole.'

Karin continued, "One year, about 1976 or 1977, we went out to the North Light on my sister's birthday, which was October 7. Our dog, Stormy, went on all of our family trips with us, all over the country. He was a mutt, a poodle mix; he looked a lot like Wallace, only in miniature. Stormy was a real climber, and he always led the way wherever we went.

"On that trip, we were climbing up the stairs to the top of the tower, as we did every year. Stormy was in front of us. My father was next in line, and he was making his usual ghost noises and joking about Foul Fellow Finnegan O'Toole.

"All of a sudden, Stormy came flying through the air! He was free-falling right past us, at a great speed. It was just a matter of seconds before we had time to realize what was happening, but miraculously, my father stretched out his arms. He was able to catch the dog, and save his life, all in just those few seconds.

"We had no explanation for the flying dog, but it became kind of a joke with us, that the ghost who lived at the North Light didn't want dogs in the tower. Either the ghost didn't like dogs, or actually did like them, and made it possible for my father to save Stormy from falling to the floor. But whether the ghost liked or disliked dogs, they definitely were not welcome in the tower.

"Ten years later, in the 1980s," Karin continued, "my dad had passed away. We were on Block Island again, and we had a new dog named Penny, the same type of dog as Stormy. The North Light was still boarded up. It was more secure than it had been, more difficult to get inside. But we had a friend, Marc Tillson." Karin hesitated, after naming the town's current Building Official. "I don't want to get Marc into trouble by mentioning him. But he had keys to the lighthouse, and we were able to go inside with him.

"It was my sister's birthday again, and this time we were in our early twenties. When we went into the lighthouse, it was still the same inside, just as haunted-looking as it had been years before, with the torn curtains and the clothes and other things from someone's life still in the closets.

"We were hiking up the stairs to the tower. Penny, the dog, was leading the way. I was next in line; my position was the same as my father's had been on our trip inside the lighthouse ten years earlier. Heidi was behind me.

"All of a sudden, Penny came flying through the air! It was just the same as when Stormy had flown through the air in that same place, ten years before. Again, it was just seconds before we realized it was happening. This time, I was able to catch Penny in mid-air, just as my father had done with Stormy a decade earlier. It was the same place on the stairs, the same everything; both times the dogs free-fell, at top speed, and both times, one of us was miraculously able to save them.

"Again, we wondered: was there some presence that did not want dogs? And if so, why was a person able to save the dogs so uncannily from falling to the floor below? My family believes that there definitely is a presence that doesn't want dogs in the tower, but it is one that likes dogs and doesn't want to see them seriously hurt.

"The first time our dog flew through the air at the North Light, it was weird," Karin Lord Carlone concluded. "But the second time — *whoa*!

"That second occasion was the last time we visited the North Light. Ten years earlier, when Stormy fell, was the last time we had been there with my father. Both of those times at the North Light were, in a sense, 'last times.'"

MYSTERY LADY AT OLD TOWN INN

"I HAVE A GHOST STORY YOU CAN USE," offered Johno Sisto, owner and proprietor of the Book Nook and Book Nook Press, as we sat at the Spring House one sunny October afternoon. We had just attended a reception for Rhode Island's governor, Don Carcieri, who was seeking re-election.

Johno, too, is a politician, wearing the hat of town leader among his many others. Having won election in 2004 — along with Governor Carcieri — Johno is now serving his first term as Second Warden of the Town of New Shoreham, after two terms as a Town Councilor.

"It was this time of year, mid to late October, about a year before Lucinda and David Morrison bought the Old Town Inn and renovated it," he recalled.

Current owners David and Lucinda Morrison bought the Inn from the former owners, the Gunthers, in November 2001 and moved in at Christmas time.

"At the time," Johno noted, "the Inn was completely closed up — I don't think it had been opened for a year or two. The plumbing was drained, the building was locked and its sign taken inside. Nobody lived there; it was just a large, empty building.

"I'd finished my work at the Book Nook, and was heading home to Old Mill Road. It was getting dark early that time of year, and it was a gray, dusky, late afternoon, about 5:30. I was driving slowly, taking my time, thinking about my plans for that night's dinner."

Johno, when he is not rewriting ordinances or sitting in council meetings, delights in culinary creativity as chef extraordinaire, regaling friends with accounts of nightly feasts, new cooking methods and recently discovered recipes. During the winter of 2004-2005, after he had put the Book Nook to bed for the season, he worked as a cook in the kitchen of the Beachead Restaurant on weekends, as well as holding down a job at the Block Island Depot most days. "I really want to learn more about commercial cooking," he told me when embarking on these latest career moves.

Continuing his ghost story, Johno described his route: "I was driving on Old Town Road, coming around the bend from Sprague Lumber with the Inn coming up on the right. As I came around the bend, I saw that a woman was walking from the front door of the Inn toward the road. I wasn't going more than 15 or 20 miles per hour, so I got a good look at her. She was dressed in what I imagine was Edwardian-era clothes — something you would see in a Masterpiece Theater series. She had brown hair pulled up in a bun, and she was wearing a white blouse with a high neck and ruffled sleeves, and a dark red jumper — the kind that's cut high up, with a neckline straight across and straps

over the shoulders. She wore black boots. She was walking very pur-
posefully with straight, measured steps, holding her hands together in
front of her and looking down. As I passed her and began slowing
down, coming up to the stop sign, she turned and started walking
toward the large horse chestnut tree that stands at the corner of the
property next to the intersection. She never took any notice of me, but
I got a really distinct impression of her appearance.

"I thought to myself, 'She's about a week early for Hallowe'en!'

"Then I realized, the Inn was empty, no one had been living there for
a year or two. That entire crossroads area was empty. There was no
sign of anyone else around, and no place nearby for anyone to go on
foot. What was she doing there?

"Well, I stopped at the intersection and looked back behind me, but
there was no one there. Yet, I'd seen her plain as day as I approached
the Inn, and watched her as I passed right by her. I immediately
thought I had just seen a ghost, but wasn't scared and drove on, probably refining my plans for dinner."

Newly renovated by the Morrisons, the ten-room Old Town Inn, built
in 1825, is a cheerful and busy year round home for Lucinda and
David Morrison and their daughters, Phoebe and Natalie. Community
pot-luck dinners, school activities, and the normal social events of an
active young family all take place here.

The horse chestnut tree in the front yard, where Johno's ghost disappeared, is very rare and is one of the oldest trees on the Island, Lucinda
told me. As for ghosts inside the building, she said with a laugh, "I've
never experienced anything here, but I would welcome it!

"The former owners, the Gunthers, had a priest come to the house at
one point to bless the house or exorcise something, I'm not sure
which," she noted. "Perhaps they had something odd happen. I'm
never afraid to be alone here, and I wish these walls could talk.
Sometimes, in case any spirits happen to be listening, I tell them, 'If
you have a party, please invite me!'"

Creepy presences at the Inn? Well, Herman Munster slept here! Said
Lucinda: "It's funny, when the Gunthers owned the Inn, the actor who
played Herman Munster on The Munsters TV series stayed here."

The Inn takes its name from its location, the crossroad that formed
Block Island's former town center. When the first white settlers from
Massachusetts arrived on the Island in 1661, they envisioned a town
on the south bank of the Great Salt Pond, with a cemetery at one end
and the cove now known as the Hog Pen at the other end. Instead, the
Island's center of commerce evolved at the crossroad where Center
Road, Old Town Road and Beacon Hill Road converge. Relatively central geographically, the crossroad became a hub for Island tradesmen
to set up shops and a tavern, and for farmers and fishermen to sell or

barter their wares on market days. The town hall, a district school, library, Baptist church, the Primitive Methodist Church, stores, a black-smith shop, cobbler shop, the town pound, and a windmill that ground corn meal, once stood in this area. Now, the Island's formerly bustling center of trade is marked by a row of antique millstones placed by the side of the road.

In the 1870s, an era of prosperity for Block Island as trades flourished and tourism grew, the rambling, welcoming structure now known as the Old Town Inn was the home and general store of Lorenzo Littlefield. Livermore's *History of Block Island*, published by the Block Island Historical Society and available at the Society's museum shop, describes Lorenzo Littlefield's home as "a fine residence, adorned with ornamental trees, walks, shrubs and flowers, and productive fruit trees…an ornament to the Island. His pond of full-blooded wild geese should be seen by visitors." Noting that "flower gardens are a recent ornament to the grounds about the houses," Livermore's 1877 publication added that "Mrs. Lorenzo Littlefield's at the Center, is very attractive in summer, and silently reminds the Islanders of the fact that God makes flowers to be seen as well as fish and vegetables to be eaten, and that Adam and Eve were first placed in a garden and commanded to 'dress it and to keep it.'"

The Morrisons are interested in restoring the grounds and gardens, as much as possible, to their former grandeur.

Lorenzo Littlefield's store was one of three at the town center at that time; the other two were owned by Alvin Sprague and William P. Ball. Much of their trade consisted of bartering for whatever might be carried through their doors: poultry, live or dressed; bags of sea moss; cheese or butter; jugs of fish oil; rags; junk; potatoes, oats and other produce; and, noted Livermore, "tons of codfish…and frequently a child with an egg in each hand."

The Morrisons have Lorenzo Littlefield's store ledger, used from 1876 to 1879, with its list of customers, transactions, goods and prices. Littlefield could buy wholesale, from Welcom Dodge, 16.78 pounds of codfish for $71.25, or four dozen eggs for $1.20. When goods were bartered, careful accounts were kept; many of Nathan Mott's purchases could be taken care of by 304 pounds of turkeys sold to Littlefield for $36.48, and 15 bushels of potatoes for $8.25. If Littlefield hadn't sufficient cash to pay for wholesale merchandise, it was duly noted in a subsequent purchase that part of a customer's bill was offset "by short pay on chickens," for example.

S.T. Livermore, author of the *History of Block Island*, was a customer. In December 1876, he bought two bushels of meal, paying the $1.50 in cash. In the spring of 1877, he bought a pair of boots and ran up a credit of $1.75. Later that month, he apparently borrowed $200 cash from

Mr. Littlefield. In July, Livermore made good on his debts with a payment of $201.75. His book on Block Island was published in 1877; perhaps sales were brisk.

Littlefield sold all manner of goods in his general store, in addition to food items: boots at $3.00 a pair; window curtains, four for 40¢; lamps at $1.50 and lampshades at 30¢; tobacco, half a pound for 35¢; a "coil of yarns" for $7.64; ten yards of calico for 80¢; a dozen buttons for 15¢; straw hats at $1.00, a box of writing paper for 25¢. And much more. Livermore noted in his history that in those days, the annual business of such a store, dealing in items plain and fancy, might amount to about $100,000 a year.

Edith Littlefield Blane, a lifelong Island resident, told me that the present Old Town Inn was, for a time, the home of Frank and Lily Littlefield and, later, of a Lester Littlefield — but not the same Lester Littlefield who is the late father of current Old Town Road resident Everett Littlefield. "There was a story," added Edith, "that somebody had pushed Lily down the stairs of the house when she died, but I don't know if that's true or not."

A fictionalized account of this rumored murder at the Old Town Inn can be found in a mystery novel entitled *Only in New England: The Story of a Gaslight Crime*, written by Theodore Roscoe and published in 1959. Roscoe calls the murder "one of the strangest unsolved murder cases in New England," citing "a former State Senator…accused of slaying his mother." The copy of Roscoe's book that I checked out of the Island Free Library had an enticing note penciled in, by a reader or a former owner, underneath the author's introduction: "Ann Elizabeth Littlefield murdered? By her son Frank Littlefield — State Senator 1911."

A GHOST WHO UNVEILS THE SUNRISE?

I'VE BEEN MEANING TO TELL YOU, I HAVE A GHOST," said Bob Pollitt to me one morning, as we met in front of the bank at Bridgegate Square. Bob, who has an old farmhouse at Dunn's Landing, is a member of the Dunn family, which has a long history on Block Island. Bob was a banker in Essex, Connecticut, before he and his late wife, Duffy, decided to move to Block Island year round. Bob has been a dedicated member of the Block Island Ecumenical Choir's tenor section and a talented song and dance man in the choir's annual variety shows. When he is not on the Island, Bob is likely to be traveling in England, Africa, South America, or on a cruise ship with his nephew, Island well driller Rick Batchelder.

After mentioning his ghost, Bob hastily added, "I mean, I don't believe in ghosts and all that stuff, but I have a door that opens itself."

I was all attention, as Bob went into more detail: "I've shaken it after closing it, I've made sure it's set right. I've put a rug in that room to keep the door from opening once it's shut. Darn thing still comes open." He added, "It's got one of those old-fashioned latches, the kind where the bar fits into a metal groove. Every time I shut the door, I try to get it open by pulling it and rattling it, but I can't get it open that way. I always make sure the latch is closed tightly. But that door always opens! Happens at night. Been doing it for years!"

"Does it open quickly or slowly?" I asked.

"I just hear a little click as the latch comes up," he replied, "and it doesn't open really wide — just slightly ajar, about four or five inches.

"The windows in the room beyond look east," he added, "so when the door is opened at night, I can see the first rays of the sun in the morning."

An old building settling? Vibrations from some external source? (Not likely, the way Bob described his own rattling of the door.) Or a gentle, benign spirit who wants Bob to awaken to a view of the sunrise?

NEW "SPIN" ON PHOTOGRAPHS AT THE OLD HYGEIA

SITUATED ON OCEAN AVENUE, atop a hill overlooking Trim's Pond, the B&B known as the Hygeia House has enjoyed a renaissance under current owners Champlin ("Champ") and Lisa Starr. The present Hygeia House was built as an annex to the Hygeia Hotel, which stood across the street on land now occupied by the police station and fire barn. Sadly, the hotel burned in 1916, but the annex survived. By 1987, when I first saw it, the fine old building had fallen on hard times. Neglected, dilapidated, falling apart, it was eventually boarded up when it was deemed a dangerously attractive nuisance. For years, the Hygeia's appearance of genteel poverty appealed to the imagination of Island resident and visitor alike. "What do the owners want for that place?" was a question frequently asked by visitors. To those whose minds and pocketbooks inclined more to the fanciful than the possibly-profitable, the Hygeia looked like a classic haunted house, whether it was or not.

The Hygeia was put on the market in the 1990s, and to the delight of Island residents, the sale turned out to be a family matter. Champ Starr, like the two Champlin brothers who bought the hotel in the 1890s, is descended from Nathaniel Champlin, who settled on the Island during the late 1700s. Related to the Starr and Champlin families are the Payne and Phelan families. When the Hygeia annex was put on the market in the 1990s, the sale was overseen by Island real estate brokers Blake and Michele Phelan. Blake Phelan and Champlin Starr are cousins. When the Starrs bought the marvelous old relic, people in the community were pleased that the Hygeia finally had prospects for a future.

During the time that the Hygeia annex was being shown as a saleable property, Johno Sisto had an odd experience while taking some onsite photos. He reported:

"When Blake and Michele Phelan were overseeing the sale of the Hygeia House, they asked me if I would like to help them clear a path through the old building so prospective bidders could walk through it safely. I jumped at the chance to view first-hand this bit of Island history and brought along my camera to possibly take a few photos. At that time, I was doing a lot of photography for *The Works* magazine."

The Works was a Block Island magazine that flourished in the 1990s and into the early 2000s. It began as an arts magazine, published monthly by Carolyn Brown and Brainard Carey, and was later taken over by Book Nook of Block Island. As *The Works* grew in size and popularity, it featured articles of historic interest, personal profiles, photo essays, poetry, crossword puzzles, book reviews, humor, recipes, and more. Continued Johno, describing the atmosphere of the long-neglected

Hygeia: "The inside was pretty cluttered. You could tell some rooms had seen evidence of squatters having "camped out" there, but other rooms looked as if no one had been in them for ages and were covered in years and years of dust.

"I had loaded up my camera with a new roll of film and brought along a flash, thinking it wouldn't be too bright inside. I was getting set to take my first picture in what I assumed was a front foyer room and as soon as the light on the flash went on, telling me it was ready, I aimed and clicked.

"The flash misfired — didn't go off at all — and I brought the camera down from my eye to check it out. Just then, the back door of the camera popped open all by itself and the new roll of film spun out of its cartridge all over the back of the now-open camera!

"This happened after my encounter with the ghost outside the Old Town Inn, so perhaps I was a little more open to the idea of ghosts. I reasoned that someone or something at the Hygeia did not want me taking pictures of the rooms when they were in such a state of disrepair, so I stuffed the exposed roll of film in my jacket pocked, put my camera in its bag, and got back to helping Blake and Michele clear a path for their customers."

DO HYGEIA HOUSE HAUNTS
HAVE AN ARTISTIC BENT?

LISA SILVERBERG STARR, published poet and busy mother, is owner/innkeeper, with her husband, Champlin Starr, of the Hygeia House. Since their purchase of the property in the 1990s and their extensive renovation of the long-neglected building, the Starrs' ownership of the Hygeia has been a labor of love. As noted in the previous story, members of the same Champlin family from which Champ Starr is descended bought the property in 1899.

Originally, the Hygeia was built as an annex to the very grand Hygeia Hotel. The main hotel, built in high Gothic Victorian style by Dr. Charles Hadley in 1886, stood on the site of the present-day police station and fire barn, at the corner of Beach and Ocean Avenues. The Hygeia was one of many luxurious Block Island hotels that catered to a wealthy clientele during the mid- to late 1800s and early 1900s. Tourists in those days came to Block Island on the great steamboats that plied the waters of the east coast. The shipping lines made Block Island a regular stop with increasing frequency. The Island had become newly fashionable as a healthful place where one could "take the waters," benefiting from sea air, ocean bathing and ingestion of the Island's pure, fresh drinking water. Block Island had the added benefits of a pleasantly cool climate and, according to promotional brochures of the period, absence of mosquitoes and biting flies.

The Hygeia was named for the ancient Greek goddess of health, and Dr. Hadley made sure his hotel had all the accommodations necessary for health and comfort. Rooms were large and airy, each with a fireplace, wash bowl, and running spring water. Hot and cold sea water and shower baths were available inside the hotel, with surf bathing nearby. Though the Hygeia's advertisements noted repeatedly that there was no malaria on Block Island and that the Island's restful atmosphere promoted healthful well-being, a physician was in attendance at the hotel in case of emergency.

In 1899, the Hygeia was enlarged and became grander than ever. It had been purchased by Senator Christopher E. Champlin and his brother, Dr. John C. Champlin; the new owners added large wings and improved the parlors and grounds to such an extent that the 250-foot-long Hygeia was considered the Island's most fashionable destination. A nine-hole golf course was added. The main hotel burned to the ground in August 1916.

Champ and Lisa opened their newly renovated Hygeia House as a bed-and-breakfast in the 1990s. Since seeing it for the first time in the 1980s, I had been fascinated by the old building and couldn't help wondering if there were ghostly presences there.

I mentioned it to Lisa Starr one day in passing. I had left a message on her phone a few days earlier, around Hallowe'en of 2004, and received no response, but when I saw her, she said with a glint in her eye, "You know, things have been happening and I think we might have something — give me a call next week!"

I did. "We have stuff happen here all the time!" she exclaimed. "We don't necessarily see a person, but when things happen, both Champ and I sit up and take notice!

"One night last winter, I was sitting in the living room, paying bills. Champ was cleaning the kitchen. Suddenly, we both heard someone sneeze, very loudly and clearly. We each knew we hadn't sneezed. Champ came into the living room and asked me if I'd sneezed, and I said no, and so we each knew the other one hadn't sneezed, either — but we both heard it.

"Then a few weeks ago, something strange happened. I've been working with a group of visual artists, and during the weekend of October 22, a group of them was here at the Hygeia. One fellow was a printmaker. He was very creative, and he wanted to incorporate our portraits into a piece of the wallpaper we had used in the Hygeia. I agreed to give him a piece of the paper.

"Champ was away that weekend, and when he came back, he asked me, 'Did you pull down the kitchen wallpaper?' We had a roll of it on a shelf, with a bunch of other things, and it had somehow come loose and fallen down. It was all by itself on the floor. It had come unrolled and there was a sixteen-inch snip out of it.

"My first thought was that maybe the print-maker had helped himself, because to tell the truth, the wallpaper had completely slipped my mind by the time the weekend was over. I e-mailed him to see if he'd taken a piece; he e-mailed back, saying he had forgotten to ask me for the paper before he left, and could I possibly mail a piece to him? I did — and the unrolled wallpaper on the floor, with a piece cut from it, remained a mystery.

"Other people have mentioned odd occurrences from time to time, too," continued Lisa. "A woman who was staying here felt a hand around her ankle one night in bed, and the chambermaids sometimes get freaked out.

"And another time, about a month ago, Champ and our son, Orrin, were in the parlor, just talking. All of a sudden the stereo came on. There was a Gordon Bok CD already in it, but it hadn't been listened to in three or four days, and it just came on by itself.

"So, it's just little things, but it definitely makes me think there's something up."

AT THE NARRAGANSETT, GHOSTS
OR NON-GHOSTS MAY HAUNT

RALLY AND I WERE HAVING DINNER at the Beachead one evening in December of 2004 with Eleanor Mott. It was a week and a half before Christmas, and the atmosphere was festive. The restaurant was busy that night, and the chefs were on their mettle; Eleanor and I both had a particularly good dish of scallops with risotto.

Eleanor and her five children — John, James, Susan, George and Peter — are the owners of the Narragansett Inn. Peter Mott's wife, Marea, incidentally, is the photographer for this volume of stories.

Built on a hill overlooking New Harbor in 1912, the Narragansett Inn, a grand old waterfront hotel, was located on land that had been farmed by the Mott family for 200 years, since their arrival on the Island in the early 1700s. A 1914 brochure for the inn described the grounds thus: "For a back ground it has a beautiful farm owned by the proprietor from which the table is supplied with vegetables, milk, chickens, eggs, etc." The Mott family built the Narragansett Inn, and they have owned it ever since.

Generations of Motts have lived, worked and graduated from school on Block Island, from their arrival here 300 years ago to the present day. Eleanor's late husband, Samuel D. Mott, was a particularly enterprising businessman and politician. In addition to owning and operating the Narragansett Inn for years with Eleanor, Sam was owner, at various times, of Smuggler's Cove and Dead Eye Dick's restaurants in New Harbor, as well as the Spring House on the other side of Old Harbor. An alumnus of Moses Brown School and Brown University, he was a hotelier and businessman all his life, and served as Block Island's representative to the Rhode Island General Assembly.

The first proprietor of the Narragansett was Sam's mother, Clossie, who ran the hotel with her daughters, Venetia and Bernice. That was back in the days when the surrounding Mott farm supplied the inn with fresh foods for the table, and hotel laundry was hung on the line to dry. Clossie personally saw to every detail of her inn and its guests; she was the major force behind the business, and it was very much a part of her. To this day, if mysterious sounds or footesteps are heard in the old building, if furniture or objects move, guests and staff will give a shrug and a nod and say, "Oh, yes, that's Clossie again."

Eleanor told me, that December evening at the Beachead, "They still say that Clossie rocks in her chair, in one of the upstairs bedrooms." Eleanor then told me of another "ghost" with origins that she knew full well.

Sam and Eleanor Mott's manager at the Narragansett Inn for many years was a man named King Odell. He started at the Narragansett in

1955, "the year Sam and I were married," said Eleanor, adding that the wedding date was May 20, just in time for the summer season. Odell came from the mainland each summer for four decades, helping the Motts run the hotel and continuing, after Sam's death, to help Eleanor and her children manage the business. A teacher at Moses Brown School on the mainland, Odell knows nine languages, Eleanor told me. "He'll never retire," she said, although in 2005 King Odell did retire, with many accolades, from his long and distiguished teaching career. He still visits the Island from time to time in the summer, usually with the senior class of Moses Brown, and on these occasions slips away from the students to enjoy a lunch with Eleanor.

Like Sam Mott, Odell was an enterprising investor who owned, at various times, the airport diner, the Empire Theatre, and the white Victorian building opposite the theater. That building is now home to the Inn at Old Harbor, Rags, Ben & Jerry's and the Water Street Café. In the days of King Odell's ownership, it housed a drugstore known as King's Spa.

"When King was at the Narragansett," Eleanor said, "there was a dapper little fisherman who used to leave his boat at the dock and stay at the hotel when he came to the Island. He was a professor, I remember. He always took the same room, on the third floor. It had a private bathroom and was actually for two people, but he liked that room and insisted on staying in it every time he came here.

"One day, King decided to play a joke on him. We used walkie-talkies to communicate with each other in those days, and King hid a walkie-talkie in the closet of that third floor room. After the professor had gone up to his room and been there awhile, a voice came from the closet: "Help! Let me out of here!" There was no one in the closet of course, and the professor ran out of that room and down to the first floor, just as white as a sheet!

"When the trick was discovered, of course, King confessed, and we all had a good laugh.

"That's the only 'ghost' I've experienced at the Narragansett — and I knew where that one came from!" Eleanor concluded.

SO WHAT WAS THAT PALATINE LIGHT?

STORIES OF THE SHIP KNOWN AS THE PALATINE have been told and written for more than two centuries. Many are documented in Reverend Samuel T. Livermore's 19th-century *History of Block Island*. I mention the *Palatine* here, certainly not because I have any first-hand accounts of this 18th-century event, but because people are intrigued by stories of shipwrecks. The *Palatine* has its own famous Island "ghost," known as the *Palatine* light, and its own poem: a vividly inaccurate ballad called *The Palatine*, penned in 1867 by John Greenleaf Whittier, that still causes Block Islanders to bristle with scorn and indignation. Any excursion into *Palatine* territory is an exercise in getting at the truth of a matter.

The *Palatine* light was a moving offshore light that people claimed to have seen as early as 1810 in various parts of Block Island Sound off Sandy Point. The light was said to resemble a square-rigged ship in flames. A written account of this phenomenon by Block Island resident Aaron C. Willey, who reported seeing the mysterious light in February and again in December of 1810, drew upon his own and other people's sightings. Willey described a light resembling a "blaze of fire," emitting "luminous rays," that rose from the ocean near Sandy Point. Neither Willey nor other eyewitnesses were sure if the light touched the water or hovered above it. It varied in size and magnitude, said Willey: "Sometimes it is small, resembling the light through a distant window, at others expanding to the highness of a ship with all her canvas spread. When large it displays a pyramidical form."

Willey quoted another eyewitness, who lived near the water and reported that when the light was within half a mile of the shore, its brightness fully illuminated the inside of his house through the window. The duration of the light's greatest and least brightness, as it moved between the two extremes, was said to be about two or three minutes.

Said Willey, of the light's movement: "After the radiance seems to be totally extinct it does not always return in the same place, but is not unfrequently seen shining at some considerable distance from where it disappeared. In this transfer of locality it seems to have no certain line of direction." The light was seen at all times of year, he noted, but mostly in calm weather preceding an easterly or southerly storm. "It is often seen blazing at six or seven miles distant, and strangers suppose it to be a vessel on fire."

He added, "From this time, it is said, the *Palatine* light appeared, and there are many who firmly believe it to be a ship of fire, to which their fantastic and distempered imaginations figure masts, ropes, and flowing sails."

Willey conjectured that the cause of the "roving brightness" could be "a peculiar modification of electricity" or the burning of flammable gas upon the water.

Decades later, toward the end of the 19th century, the Reverend Mr. Livermore came up with the idea that the blazing light might result from gases that had escaped from petroleum deposits on the ocean floor. Upon reaching the surface of the water, the gases burst into flames, possibly ignited by lightning. This theory was advanced again in the 1960s by a U.S. government geologist.

Another explanation was offered in the 1880s by Rhode Island historian Welcome A. Greene, after a night fishing expedition. Greene theorized that the blaze of light came from large schools of menhaden, a particularly oily, phosphorescent species of fish.

There were those, however, who clung to the idea that the moving, offshore light was associated with the *Palatine*, the name commonly assigned to a ship that was said to have gone aground at the hummock off Sandy Point in the 1700s. After Whittier's 1867 poem, *The Palatine*, was published, the popular imagination soared with the notion that the mysterious light was the ghostly *Palatine* itself, in flames, returning after a grisly shipwreck to haunt the scene of its demise.

Block Islanders have always taken serious issue with Whittier's poem, which describes the wreck of the *Palatine* in very colorful and utterly fictitious terms. In his ballad, Whittier maligned Block Islanders who were present at the *Palatine* grounding as "wreckers," who, having lured the ship to its doom with false lights, swooped down "like birds of prey, tearing the heart of the ship away," plundering, murdering all on board, then setting fire to the ruined vessel and casting it adrift.

A 19th-century Rhode Islander named Benjamin Congdon, who claimed to have seen the blazing *Palatine* light ten times, tied the light, the shipwreck and Whittier's poem together in a moralistic explanation typical of the time: "The crime was a little more than the Almighty could stand, so He sent the Fire or Phantom Ship to let them know He had not forgotten their wickedness. She was seen once a year, on the same night of the year on which the murder occurred."

To the present day, Block Island residents have little use for Whittier or his poem. As the late, legendary Maizie Lewis, taxi driver, author, and Island tour guide, told a journalist in 1960, "Whittier was a character assassin." She dubbed *The Palatine* "the cruelest poem ever written."

Historic accounts of the actual shipwreck vary, including controversy as to the name of the ship, the date, and whether it was actually wrecked. Livermore believed that the supposedly wrecked ship was indeed called the *Palatine*. One of his sources, an Islander and scholar named Charles E. Perry, placed the time of the shipwreck at about 1752. After extensive interviews with Island residents whom he con-

112

sidered reliable purveyors of the stories handed down through their families, Livermore maintained that not only was the *Palatine* not burned, it in fact was wrecked in the Bay of Bengal in July 1784, according to records of the Dutch Trading Society. Stripping superstition and poetry from the *Palatine* stories, Livermore concluded that a ship called *Palatine*, a Dutch trading ship, had come to Block Island in the mid-1700s, left many diseased and dying passengers on the Island, then continued on its journey. The passengers, he maintained, received only the kindest treatment from the Island's inhabitants.

In his *History of Block Island*, Livermore references an account by Islander Benjamin Sprague, who remembered his parents talking about the ship *Palatine* and one of its survivors, a woman known as "Dutch Kattern." Kattern, who lived on Corn Neck, told people that the ship's crew had starved the passengers to get their money. She was reported to be a fortune-teller, and thought by many to be a witch; there were accounts that she habitually went outside her house to lie in a trance for hours at a time, returning home exhausted and reporting out-of-body excursions to her home in Holland. Sprague himself knew Kattern's daughter, Cradle, whose father was a black man whom Kattern had married after arriving on the Island.

Other authorities, before and since, have maintained that the word "*Palatine*" refers to the ship's passengers, who were thought to have been German Protestant refugees from the ancient German districts known as the Upper and Lower Palatinates. Rhode Island shipping records, while fixing the exact date of the wreck as December 27, 1738, also indicate that no ship called the *Palatine* had ever crossed the Atlantic at a time to coincide with that date. However, in 1738, the *Princess Augusta*, a 220-ton merchant ship from Ramsgate, England, stopped at Rotterdam to take on 350 Palatine emigrants. A rich ship with a cargo valued at 20,000 pounds sterling, she was bound for Philadelphia.

Records verify only three of the *Princess Augusta's* passengers: a wealthy woman named Mary Van der Line who was carrying a lot of gold and silver; and two women named Kattern, one tall and one short. The two were called Long Kattern and Short Kattern; Long Kattern later became known on Block Island as Dutch Kattern, a fortune-teller and fantasy-weaver.

The *Princess Augusta* was doomed from the start of her voyage. She was carrying drinking water that had been polluted by mold from casks previously used to store wine. After a short time at sea, 300 crew and passengers became ill, and only 114 recovered. Among the dead buried at sea were the captain and seven of his crew.

Under the command of the first mate, Andrew Brook, the *Princess Augusta* had a long and arduous crossing, beset by gales and suffering dwindling food supplies and a severe shortage of potable water. Corroborating tales that Dutch Kattern was later to tell Block Islanders, records of the voyage indicated that Brook and his crew threatened passengers with starvation to get money and valuables from them.

On December 19th, when Brook sighted land, he thought he was near Maryland. He was actually off the tip of Long Island. After several days of rough weather, he got his bearings and decided to head for Rhode Island. Sighting the mainland, he hoisted a distress signal but got no response. He headed south, toward Philadelphia, with heavy snow obscuring visibility and fierce winds carrying the *Princess Augusta* toward Block Island.

At 2:00 p.m. on December 27th, the ship struck the hummock off the north end of Block Island's Sandy Point. A plank ripped from the hull, and she took on water. The ill and weakened Palatine passengers tried to go over the sides to get ashore, but were stopped by Brook.

It was First Warden Simon Ray, 85 years old at the time, who persuaded Brook to loose the sheet anchor so the ship would not be carried away on the tides. Islanders then secured the *Princess Augusta* with a cable and helped the passengers ashore. Brook offered no aid. He forbade the passengers from taking their possessions, and refused to distribute the remaining bread to them. Instead, he lugged his own sea chest off the ship. On December 28th, Brook ordered the cable unhitched, and the *Princess Augusta* drifted away with the passengers' belongings. Outraged Block Islanders pursued the vessel and were able to save 20 chests, which were restored to their owners.

Charles E. Perry's research into the Palatine shipwreck indicated that all passengers, except for one woman who insisted on staying with the ship, were brought ashore by the Block Islanders who went to their aid. Records show that on December 29th, when the *Princess Augusta* was last seen off the Island's west side, the wealthy Mary Van der Line was still on board. She had refused to leave her belongings behind, though why she was not simply removed, herself, remains a mystery. She went down with the ship, which smashed to pieces on a rock. Nobody set fire to the vessel.

In his 19th-century account, Livermore pooh-poohs the notion of setting fire to a ship: "Her timbers and irons were too valuable to the Islanders to be wasted. Certain it is that the strict laws of the Island would have duly punished the known incendiary, had he been a citizen."

A prominent 20th-century Island resident, Lester Dodge, echoed this practical sentiment to a reporter in the 1960s: "Burn a shipwreck? They'd as likely burn the roofs over their heads. Timber was too scarce." Dodge, who upon his death bequeathed funds to build the

Island Free Library, was descended from Island settler Trustrum Dodge. Lester Dodge confessed to a secret fondness for Whittier's poem, strictly on literary grounds, and could reel off the verses from memory — but he scoffed at Whittier's version of the shipwreck as pure nonsense.

A word about "wreckers": like other coastal-dwelling people the world over, Block Islanders have, for centuries, salvaged shipwrecks, recycling timbers and making use of cargoes that would otherwise be lost. This is done by pre-arrangement with ship owners, by which salvagers are granted a share of what is recovered. It is a practical arrangement that benefits salvagers and owners alike, and is not to be confused with the evil practice of luring a ship to its doom for the purpose of plunder, as described by Whittier.

One hundred of the original 350 Palatines who left Rotterdam made it to Block Island. Survivors were taken to the houses of Edward Sands and Simon Ray; the latter owned a large tract of land on the Island's west side. The Palatine passengers were well cared for, but twenty died, some from exposure and some from the after-effects of illness and starvation. Long Kattern and Short Kattern stayed on the Island, while others went to the mainland, bound for Philadelphia.

One woman who survived, wrote Charles Perry, gave to Edward Sands's little daughter a dress of India calico. The little Sands girl grew up to become the grandmother of Charles Perry's grandmother, and she often told first-hand accounts of this story to her family. Long, or Dutch, Kattern married a slave belonging to the Littlefield family and had three children. (Generations later, Kattern's great-great grandson, Jack, was employed by the Honorable Nicholas Ball as a handy man at the famous Ocean View Hotel.) Dutch Kattern had the reputation of telling fanciful (and destructive) tales of the shipwreck she had experienced, embellishing her stories with details of plunder, murder and arson. These tales eventually became part of the lore and legend surrounding the ship.

The Palatines who died were buried west of the house of William P. Lewis in the southwest part of the Island, at the site now known as the Palatine Graves. In 1947, the Block Island Historical Society placed a memorial marker at the graves.

So — what was, or is, the legendary Palatine light? No one seems to know, and no recent sightings have been reported. Livermore concluded that overly-active imaginations were responsible for "rigging the light off Sandy Point with masts, ropes, and sails, and for giving it a cargo of lies to feed the fancies of poets, and the phantom-chasers of posterity. Dutch Kattern had her revenge on the ship that put her ashore by imagining it on fire, and telling others, probably, that the light on the sound was the wicked ship Palatine, cursed for leaving her on Block Island."

In the mid-20th century, as Block Island became an increasingly busy destination for vacationers, "eyewitness" accounts of the light cropped up, particularly in the summer months. Whatever else the light might (or might not) have been, Island residents quickly recognized that it was an aid to tourism.

The late Samuel Mott, Block Island representative to the Rhode Island General Assembly, owner of the Narragansett Inn, and owner for many years of the Spring House, attested in 1960 to three sightings: "Each time she came was on a black winter night. She'd pass the Point moving fast, a regular floating bonfire. Then down she'd sink back into the deep," he deadpanned.

Another authority of the day was the late Clarence Lewis, then owner of the Lewis Farm. Situated next to Southwest Point, the farm had been acquired by his great-grandfather in 1817:

"First time I seen her, maybe fifty years ago," he said earnestly in the 1960s, describing his vision of the Palatine light, "I was standing on our front stoop with my ma and pa. My pa, he hollers, 'That's her, that's the light!' And he tells how she's always followed by a sou'easter. Sure enough, a couple of hours later, the heaviest one I ever recall blows up."

And thus do tales continue.

WHERE THE DEAD HAVE SETTLED

THE GHOSTS OF BLOCK ISLAND seem to enjoy a parallel existence with living souls. They haunt the spaces occupied by live people, and their haunting habits are, for the most part, gentle and non-threatening. My husband Rally maintains that ghosts cannot hurt people and I've certainly never heard of injury or death by ghost, but: would one hear of it if it did occur?

Ghosts seem to be souls that have not found peaceful rest in a realm separated from the living, and the reasons for their activities and behavior usually remain a mystery to those whom they haunt. Yet, ghosts continue to manifest themselves among the living in various ways, presumably to send a message of their restlessness. Perhaps ghosts are trying to be helpful to the living. Or, they may be having a dull day in "ghostdom," and feel an urge to tease the bulky mortals who now live among them.

It should come as no great surprise, therefore, that encounters with ghosts at the Island Cemetery have not been reported. Most collections of ghost tales include at least one midnight meeting with a graveyard ghost: a swirling specter emanating from underneath a headstone, perhaps, or a faceless, shrouded figure that stalks among the graves; a grisly hand that points accusingly at a murderer, or invisible fingers that clutch at those who traverse a graveyard at night; a hollow laugh that chills the bones of even the bravest of children, or a wailing voice of despairing unrest that is heard at full moon.

But this ghost story collection has none of those.

Why, after all, would a ghost haunt a cemetery? Except for occasional visitors, there are no living people there to receive a message. Cemeteries are places of rest for the dead, not places of opportunity for restless spirits of the dead.

Nevertheless, a cemetery contains plenty of "living spirits," in the form of records of those who have gone before, and have left their mark on a place: in this case, Block Island. Here are names, dates and achievements. Here are sentiments carved in stone by grief-stricken survivors, and monument designs ranging from the ornate to the starkly enigmatic or even the utilitarian. Here are the intertwinings of founding families' surnames with other prominent Island names as marriages took place, and here are family regroupings due to second marriages and second families. This rich legacy of information, of messages to the living concerning those souls who seem to have found peaceful rest, is presented in a variety of styles that reflect the tastes and the means of those who have used the Island Cemetery over the centuries of its existence.

The location of the Island Cemetery was chosen by the white settlers who arrived here from Massachusetts in 1661. Those settlers envisioned a town on the shore of the Great Salt Pond, with a cemetery at the west end of town.

The town never grew next to the Great Salt Pond, due to the seeming impossibility of digging a lasting channel that would transform the pond into a harbor. Instead, the crossroads that is now the corner of Center Road, Beacon Hill Road and Old Town Road became the Island's first commercial center.

The cemetery, however, on its ten-acre hill, took hold as intended by the early settlers. It also became the site of a Baptist meetinghouse in 1814. Interestingly, construction of the meetinghouse was aided by Commodore Hardy, commander of the British blockading squadron on patrol here during the war of 1812. Block Island took a neutral stance in the war and was therefore not an adversary to the British. In the 1850s, the meetinghouse was moved to the commercial center. Used as a town hall and a high school, it was destroyed on Halloween night in 1923 by a fire of unknown origin.

The cemetery evolved, for the most part, in a westerly direction. The oldest section is the hillside to the left of the entrance off West Side Road, the east-facing slope, painstakingly terraced by early settlers at a time when backhoes and bulldozers were as yet undreamed. Here are the graves of the 16 families from Massachusetts who settled here in 1661. At the crown of the hill are stones dating from the 18th and 19th centuries; the western slope, and farther reaches beyond, contain relatively recent graves and many plots as yet unused.

The oldest gravestone found in the cemetery is that of Margret Gutry (or "Gvtry,"as it is carved on the stone), who died in 1687 at age 64. Trustrum Dodge, however, who died in 1683 at age 76, is also buried here. His descendant, Lester E. Dodge, replaced Trustrum's original headstone with a larger replica in the twentieth century.

Block Island's cemetery, besides being a vantage point from which to enjoy long distance views across the Island, is a treasure trove of information for historians, genealogists, artists, sculptors and anyone else intrigued by the determined settlement of this tiny Island so isolated, those three and a half centuries ago, from other land masses.

Many of the given names engraved on the stones here are unusual, little used in modern times. Ackurs, Tiddemon, Ambrose, Weeden, Waity, Tamar, Barzillai, Icivilla, Rosina, Iola, Edrianna, Hephzibah, Seraphina, Philamin Galusha, Almedie, Lot, Bersheba, Darius, Welcome, Desire, Mercy, Wealthy, Elphege and Cirlor, for example, resound with poetry, pride and character.

There are reminders of the fragility of life on an isolated island and at a time when illness or infection might not readily meet with a cure. Many stones indicate deaths of infants or children and deaths of husbands or, more often, wives, at young ages. There are deaths by drowning, reflecting the constant risk of going to sea, as people living on an island did with great frequency. And, as everywhere, there are deaths from wars. Veterans from all wars are honored every year by members of Block Island's American Legion post, who place new flags on their graves on Memorial Day and Veterans' Day.

Some people in Block Island's early years were surprisingly long-lived, by the standards of their own time and by today's standards as well. Trustrum Dodge, born in 1607, lived to the age of 76; Edward Ball 2nd, in the following century, died in 1796 at age 70. James Sands, his grave covered by a slab of red sandstone, died in 1695 at age 73. Simon Ray, born in 1635, died in 1737 at the age of 102! His son, bearing the same name, lived to be 85 and was buried in 1755.

Great diversity is shown in the materials and styles of monuments placed in the Island Cemetery over the centuries. Margret Gutry's early monument was of sandstone, and so were those of two members of the Sands family, placed in 1695 and 1708. After that, slate became the stone of choice. Three generations of Newport carvers, all named John Stevens, carved many of these, on Block Island and elsewhere in the country. Their work is characterized by primitive style carved faces, framed by wings, at the top of the stones.

By the late 18th century, brown sandstone from Connecticut was being used with great frequency for markers. Winged faces still decorated the stones, but so, now, did dramatically bent-over weeping willows. Half a century later, white marble came into vogue, and decoration became more elaborate and more diverse: crosses, ivy and floral wreaths and anchors all began to appear. Later still, around the 1860's, granite came into favor. Today, it is still the most frequently used material. New shapes arose: obelisks, spires, tiered turrets, as well as solid blocks with combinations of rough and polished surfaces. Decorations, often in high relief, reflected the carver's art: clasped hands, a hand holding a bouquet, a cross in a bed of roses, cross and crown, cherubs, doves, lambs, a cord and tassel motif. And often, as befits an island, ships and anchors. A life-size bust of the deceased, the only one of its kind in the cemetery, tops the Italian marble monument of Charles W. Willis, owner of the Surf Hotel, who died in 1892.

Noteworthy is the prominent grave marker of Nicholas Ball, at the crest of the hill to the left of the entrance road. The tall and imposing monument, surmounted by a polished black granite globe of the earth, is impossible to miss. Nicholas Ball was one of Block Island's most successful citizens, a world traveler who went to California during the 1849 gold rush, made a fortune in shipping, and took a leading role in negotiating construction of the Old Harbor breakwater, the Southeast Lighthouse, the Island's life-saving stations, and a signal station. He built and owned the Ocean View Hotel, grandest of all the Island hotels, frequented by Supreme Court justices and a U.S. president. Nicholas Ball's gravestone has an anchor to represent his career at sea (starting as a cabin boy and rising through the ranks to ship owner); a pick and shovel indicating his days as a California gold miner; a book for his scholarship and writing; and the globe, denoting his travels around the world.

Next to Nicholas Ball's grave is a very pretty little white headstone, that of his daughter-in-law, Alice Ophelia (another lovely name), who died at age 29. Her husband, Cassius Clay Ball, subsequently married the longer-lived and public-spirited Lucretia Mott. The tombstone of Cassius Clay and Lucretia Mott Ball, a blocky structure reminiscent of Empire, occupies its own curbed enclosure on the other side of Nicholas Ball's monument. Wrote Martha Ball, the town's former First Warden and the great-granddaughter of Cassius Clay and Alice Ophelia Ball, in her 1993 book, *Island Notes*, "My father's…generation held Cassius and the second wife in disdain for abandoning Alice, leaving the woman who died so young alone, forever in the shadow of her august father-in-law."

Modern grave markers in the Island Cemetery are rendered in all shapes, sizes, styles and materials. Some are of black slate, notably that of Francis Sprague, whose 18th century-style monument was carved and decorated simply, in gold leaf, by his daughter-in-law, master stone carver Karin Sprague. Some are more structural: stone altars, or, with increasing frequency, benches that welcome the visitor to sit. A single heart-shaped stone for a husband and wife, or intertwined hearts carved on a stone can be found, along with majestic and rough-hewn monoliths, simple Island boulders and Celtic crosses. Anchors and a square rigger in full sail decorate the large rectangular monument of Capt. Raymond H. Abell. George Brown, buried at sea in 1962, is memorialized by a large anchor and line carved in high relief.

Epitaphs provide insight into the ways in which survivors remember their dead, with a nod to verbal and philosophical styles of each era. Simon Ray, the settler who died in 1737 at 102 years of age, is memorialized by an unstinting, forthright list of his achievements and merits. The reader also learns that

"He was deprived of his eyesight many years
Cheerfully submitting to the will of God
His life being in this trying instance
As in all others
A lovely example of Christian virtue."

The gravestone of Elizabeth Sands, a young wife who died at age 19 in 1765, includes this admonition:

"Stop reader spend a mournful tear
Upon the dust that slumbers here

> And while you read the state of me
> Think on the glass that runs for thee."

The 1755 monument of William Greffeth, of sandstone with a winged face, tells the reader that the deceased, born in 1715, "was drowned at Block Island" in October, 1755, "aged 40 years."

Lydia R. Mott, who died at age 35 in 1877, received this tribute from grieving family:

> "We miss thee when the morning dawns,
> We miss thee when the night returns,
> We miss thee here, we miss thee there,
> Lydia we miss thee everywhere."

Mrs. Caty Mott, who died in 1814, is remembered affectionately as "the amiable consort to Lot Mott."

In more recent times, epitaphs tend to be simpler, reflecting something specific to the life of the departed, and his or her contribution to Block Island. One example is the gravestone of Jim Kelley, who sang and played piano for many years at Ballard's Inn. The stone sports a carving of a grand piano, gracefully flanked by musical notes, with the epitaph, "And the tour ends here," referring to his popular "Island tour" song.

The late Joan Abrams, owner and guiding force behind the Hotel Manisses and The 1661 Inn, is memorialized by a granite marker incised simply with a Star of David and an outline of Block Island, in recognition of her many contributions to her religious community and the greater Island community. A graceful stone angel, with clasped hands, has been placed at the base of her monument.

There are many spirits of the departed, and of those whom they influenced by their lives and works, in evidence at the Island Cemetery. In that sense, there are ghostly presences aplenty but no ghostly hauntings that I know of.

WHEN THE BECK HOUSE
BECAME LYNN'S WAY...

IN 2003, THE OLD HOUSE AT SANDS FARM, once owned by Rally's mother-in-law, Jean Beck, was bought by the Walsh family. Suzann and Frank Walsh, who summered on Block Island for years with their four children, always wanted to own a house on Block Island, but never thought they would be able to. Suzann's late sister, Lynn, in particular, was drawn to the Island and wanted to live here. After her death, the family came to Block Island to scatter her ashes from the top of Mohegan Bluffs.

"The wind blew the ashes back in, right in the direction of this house," Suzann told me. "It was as if Lynn was pointing the way to us."

After scattering the ashes, the family had a cookout on the beach near the Coast Guard station. Lynn's son, Matthew Nyberg, his wife Beth, and their two children were there. As the family was leaving the beach, the Nybergs' five-year-old daughter, Hannah, said suddenly, "Mom, I see Nene! She's right there, in the car!" Nene was the children's name for their grandmother, Lynn.

Said Suzann Walsh's daughter, Kelly, who told me this story, "It was so innocent, so real, that Hannah would tell us what she saw. At that age, children don't know they might be seeing something that no one else can see."

Shortly after that, the family decided to take a large leap and buy the former Beck House, on Block Island, from then-owner Rob Helterline. "A lot of us started talking together, to see if there was any way we could make it happen," partner John Kempf said, during a get-together at the house in December 2004. "If there hadn't been so many of us, there was no way it could have been done. But we all got together, and chipped in, and worked on it, and here we are!" They bought the house in a partnership involving eight family members and two close friends.

The Walshes are enterprising and determined, and blessed with a number of multitalented family members and friends. Suzann Walsh, who has a background in home loans, owns SMW Investment Group, a company involved in the purchase, renovation and sale of houses. She and her husband, Frank, are both involved in this business.

Other partners and family members are professionals in electrical work, plumbing, heating and refrigeration. All are adept at design and carpentry. Daughter Kelly, a musician whose band plays on the Island in the summer, is also a yoga instructor. Kelly's sister, Keri Johnson, is an interior designer and busy mother to sons Jack and Andrew. She divides her time between Block Island and her home in Florida.

Melissa, fiancée of Kelly and Keri's brother, John Walsh, is a therapeutic masseuse. John Walsh is a chef who owned the Providence Bookstore Café in Wayland Square for ten years, while his brother, Philip Walsh, was a chef at the elegant Chandler House in Newport. When on Block Island, Philip tends bar at the Albion Pub.

Chris Collins, another partner, lives in Texas. Formerly a bartender at Providence Bookstore Café, he became a close family friend and started summering out here with his two daughters. His business is real estate investments.

Lynn's son and daughter, Matthew and Michele Nyberg, are also partners. They live in Florida, where they have a construction company. Matthew Nyberg and Frank Walsh, between the two of them, oversaw the entire renovation project for the house. Michele Nyberg is an accountant, and does all the financial work for Lynn's Way.

In short, the Walshes have all the talents, business savvy, and more, needed to keep a work crew going and completely renovate an old house seriously in need of restructuring, remodeling, redecorating, and just plain tender loving care. The group worked tirelessly on the house, late into the night, for ten solid months; every single person took an active part in demolishing, designing, installing, rebuilding, sheetrocking, taping, flooring, refinishing, porch-building, and all the other down-and-dirty, hands-on tasks that needed doing. And, they are all still the best and closest of friends.

The result of all this labor, unveiled at an open house in the summer of 2004, is Lynn's Way: a large, warm, welcoming house, named for Suzann's late sister. Boasting a new second floor deck, gourmet kitchen, five or six bedrooms and a path to Sands Pond, the lovingly restored and decorated farmhouse is rented during summers and holidays, and used by the Walshes the rest of the time.

The many partners bring their diverse talents to bear when using the house themselves. On New Year's Eve in 2004, they hosted a small, spur-of-the-moment wedding reception at the house. In preparation, Caren and John Kempf combed the Island for greens to hang while researching outdoor wedding sites. Caren created a masterpiece of a wedding cake with layers baked in different sizes of cans, and the *hors d'oeuvres* offered by the two chefs in the family were plentiful and delicious. The Walshes and their hospitality are characterized by enthusiasm and resourcefulness, as was the remodeling of the house.

"We have a bunch of free spirits here," Suzann Walsh told me with a deep laugh. "It keeps things interesting!"

While the renovation of the Walshes' house was taking place in the winter of 2003 and 2004, I sometimes mused to Rally, "I wonder where the ghosts will go. Maybe," I added hopefully, "they'll come down to our house!"

"The ghosts will stay," he said with conviction. "They don't move when things get renovated; they'll probably like their new home!"

Daughters Kelly and Keri Walsh, both with long blonde hair and winning smiles, waitressed at the Beachead during the fall and winter of 2004 while living in their family's house. Keri told me that she had never had any odd or unexplainable experiences in the house. "But I'd like to!" she added.

In November 2004, just before Thanksgiving, I called Suzann Walsh, then on the mainland visiting family members. The Walshes had spent months working in their Block Island house, then living in the finished masterpiece. They had a more intimate acquaintance with every nail and board in the building than anyone in recent memory, so I reasoned that they had had ample opportunity to feel, hear or see ghostly presences — if any remained on the premises.

"Last year," Suzann told me, "when all of us were at the house, my brother, Philip Morgan, was staying in the map room. One night he was falling asleep, and he felt a presence in the room. And then, he felt the end of his mattress go down, as if someone was sitting on it. He said, 'I don't know who you are, but I hope you're friendly, because I like company.' Whatever it was, it didn't bother him."

The map room, a front northwest bedroom on the second floor, is so named because a former owner, Colonel Hart, put a huge world map all over one wall so he could keep track of World War II. Colonel Hart met his death in the house, falling down the stairs after suffering a heart attack. The map room is also next to the room where Island carpenter John Fournier saw a woman's apparition one summer when he stayed there for a few weeks.

When the Beck family owned the house, and when the Walshes bought it, Colonel Hart's map still took up that entire wall. During renovation, the Walshes replaced the wall (as they did most of the walls in the house), but kept the tradition of the map room by adding a new map. After telling me the story about her brother Philip, Suzann put her husband, Frank, on the phone. "I was sleeping downstairs one evening," he told me. "I thought our son, Philip, had come in, because I heard someone come through the door and go upstairs — but he told me the next day, he hadn't come in the previous night."

On New Year's Eve 2004, at the small wedding reception that the Walshes hosted in their dining room, John Kempf described an experience he had had during the time the family was working on the house. He was in the dining room with his sister and her husband, Nancy and Michael Hines. "We heard the door open, and we saw a shadow in the hall and heard footsteps going up the stairs," he said. "There was no mistaking any of those things, and we all heard and saw them.

"A little later, I went up to the second floor to use the bathroom, and I heard footsteps above me, on the third floor. Again, they were unmistakable. But there was nobody on the second floor. I went back downstairs. We thought maybe some other family members had come home and were up on the third floor.

"But a few hours later, those family members came home. They hadn't come in previously, and there was nobody at all on either of those upper floors. But three of us knew what we had heard. That front door definitely opened, and something or someone went up those stairs!"

John's wife, Caren Kempf, added, "I'm very happy to see that the ghosts are still here. We have a theory that Lynn, Suzann's sister, made a connection with the spirits who were here, and perhaps brought others to this place as well. The presences here seem very good, very positive."

EPILOGUE

PEOPLE HAVE OFTEN ASKED ME if I believe in ghosts, or spirits. Of course I do. Believing is believing; believing is not necessarily seeing.

While I draw the line at flaming square-riggers, I certainly believe in the existence of things that cannot be explained by rational means. I am always willing to believe in something, even an entire world or parallel universe, beyond my sight or comprehension. Or in supernatural powers or occurrences. I've never experienced a ghost firsthand, but that does not mean they do not exist. Other people have their stories.

The not-knowings, not-understandings, and not-endings are part of the mystery of life, the things that keep us all guessing.

Why would one opt not to believe in ghosts?

BIBLIOGRAPHY

Historical and factual material that appears in this book was drawn from the author's own previously published writings that appeared, over a number of years, in *The Block Island Times, The Block Island Magazine and Travel Guide,* and *The Works.*
The following sources were also consulted, and were of great value in writing this book:

• *Block Island Lore and Legends,* by Ethel Colt Ritchie, F. Norman Associates, Block Island, Rhode Island, 1955.
• *Block Island: The Land,* by Robert M. Downie, Book Nook Press, Block Island, Rhode Island, 1999.
• *Block Island: The Sea,* by Robert M. Downie, Book Nook Press, Block Island, Rhode Island, 1998.
• *Block Island Summer,* by Elizabeth and Klaus Gemming, The Chatham Press, Inc., Riverside, Connecticut, 1972.
• "Block Island, R.I. and Its Attractions," Geo. W. Richardson, 198 Broadway, New York, pub. between 1903 and 1916, exact date unknown.
• *Exploring Old Block Island,* by Herbert S. Whitman, Chatham Press, Old Greenwich, Connecticut, 1980.
• Guest Register, M.M. Day et al., in use at Connecticut House, 1878-1890s.
• *Historic and Architectural Resources of Block Island, Rhode Island,* Rhode Island Historical Preservation Commission, Providence, Rhode Island, 1991.
• *History of Block Island,* by Samuel T. Livermore, originally printed 1877, published by The Block Island Committee of Republication, Block Island, Rhode Island, 1961.
• *Images of America: Block Island,* by Donald A. D'Amato and Henry A.L. Brown, Arcadia Publishing, Charleston, South Carolina, 1999.
• *Island Notes,* by Martha Ball, The Block Press, Block Island, Rhode Island, 1993.
• Ledger, Lorenzo Littlefield, in use at his general store, April 27, 1876 to April 19, 1879.
• *New Shoreham, Rhode Island: Three Centuries of Progress, 1661-1961,* Block Island, Rhode Island, June 1961.
• *Research, Reflection and Recollections of Block Island,* by Frederick J. Benson, Block Island, Rhode Island, 1977.
• "The Highview Inn Murals," by Lisa Silverberg, *The Works,* August 1994.
• "The Mystery of the Palatine Light," by John Kobler, published in *The Saturday Evening Post,* 1960, exact date unknown.

- *Victorian Resorts and Hotels: A Victorian Society Book*, ed. Richard Guy Wilson, published as Nineteenth Century, Vol. 8, Nos. 1-2, by The Victorian Society in America, 1982.
- *Works In Progress V: From Houdini to Whodunit*, The Block Island Writers' Workshop, Block Island, Rhode Island, 1988.

ABOUT THE AUTHOR

Frances Huggard Migliaccio grew up in Worthington, Ohio. She graduated from Wheaton College in Norton, Massachusetts, and earned a Master of Arts in Teaching from Simmons College. She lived and worked in the Boston area as an editor and writer for 18 years before venturing south to Block Island. She and her husband, Rally, manage the Block Island Boat Basin, a marina for transient boaters, in New Harbor. They also own a taxi called Mig's Rig, offering regular taxi service and tours of the Island. With their black cat, named Kukla, Fran and Rally live year round on Block Island.

Previously published works include poetry, travel articles and essays in *The Christian Science Monitor* and *Yankee* magazine, articles published in *The Block Island Times* over a period of 17 years, and articles in *The Block Island Magazine and Travel Guide, Captain's Guide, The Works* magazine, the *Block Island Beacon, Natural New England,* and *Works In Progress V: From Houdini to Whodunit,* published by The Block Island Writers' Workshop. This is her first book.

For information on ordering additional copies of this book,
write to

Frances Huggard Migliaccio
att: Ghosts of Block Island
P.O. Box 412
Block Island, RI 02807